W9-CLB-400

John Osborne

Twayne's English Authors Series

TEAS 389

JOHN OSBORNE
(1929–   )
Courtesy of Redfern Gallery, London

John Osborne

By Arnold P. Hinchliffe

Manchester University

Twayne Publishers • Boston

John Osborne

Arnold P. Hinchliffe

Published by Twayne Publishers
A Division of G. K. Hall & Company
70 Lincoln Street
Boston, Massachusetts 02111

Book Production by John Amburg

Book Design by Barbara Anderson

Printed on permanent/durable acid-free
paper and bound in the United States of
America.

Library of Congress Cataloging in Publication Data

Hinchliffe, Arnold P., 1930–
John Osborne.

(Twayne's English authors series; TEAS 389)
Bibliography: p. 144
Includes index.
1. Osborne, John, 1929– —Criticism
and interpretation. I. Title. II. Series.
PR6065.S18Z68 1984 822′.914 83-13001
ISBN 0-8057-6875-0

Contents

About the Author
Preface
Acknowledgments
Chronology

Chapter One
Look Back in Anger 1

Chapter Two
The Entertainer 26

Chapter Three
The Lesson of History 49

Chapter Four
Plays for England 61

Chapter Five
Inadmissible Evidence 71

Chapter Six
For the Mean Time 89

Chapter Seven
A Sense of Detachment 107

Chapter Eight
Odd Jobs 116

Chapter Nine
A Talent to Vex 131

Notes and References 133
Selected Bibliography 144
Index 151

About the Author

Arnold P. Hinchliffe was born in 1930 at Dewsbury (Yorkshire) and educated at Ossett Grammar School. After serving two years in the Royal Engineers he went to Manchester University, where he took a First Class Honors Degree in English Literature. In 1955 he graduated from Manchester as M.A. and left for the United States. He spent a year as English Speaking Union Fellow at Yale and received an M.A. from the American Studies Department. Returning to teach in the Department of English at Manchester University he completed his Ph. D. in 1963 on symbolism in the American novel. Since then he has turned his attention to British drama. He is now Senior Lecturer in English Literature at Manchester University. His other books include a study of Harold Pinter in the Twayne English Authors Series, two volumes in "The Critical Idiom" series, *The Absurd* (which has been translated into Greek, Japanese, Korean and Arabic) and *Modern Verse Drama*, a Casebook on T. S. Eliot's *The Waste Land* (co-edited with C. B. Cox), a Casebook on Drama Criticism, *Drama Criticism: Developments Since Ibsen,* and a study of recent British Theatre, *British Theatre: 1950–1970.* He has just completed a Casebook on Eliot as Dramatist.

Preface

In 1980, shortly after the death of David Mercer, John Osborne photocopied a letter from Mercer complaining about the critical treatment of his latest plays and expressing fears that the RSC would no longer want to stage them. A copy of this letter was sent to every critic with the terse comment: R.I.P. The implication was that Mercer had been driven to an early grave by the critics. Osborne's dislike of critics has never wavered and he has not been particularly well served by them. As Simon Trussler points out, apart from "first night notices and gobbets of gossip" the writer most associated with new-wave drama has received scant critical attention. Osborne "repels criticism almost as strongly as he declares himself repelled by critics," which, Trussler suggests, is probably because of the forthrightness of his plays. Thus, his works offer no such tempting ambiguities or pregnant pauses as Pinter's; neither is his craftsmanship so careful or his sectional following so devoted as Arden's. His plays, good and bad alike, appeal to the emotions rather than the intellect.[1]

Trussler hoped that his assessment of the plays would help to stimulate "a serious critical debate about Osborne—even if it serves only negatively as a sounding-board for dissent."[2] Trussler's *The Plays of John Osborne,* published in 1969, seemed to be part of such a debate. Ronald Hayman's short study *John Osborne* had appeared in 1968 and in 1969 Trussler had also contributed the British Council Pamphlet on Osborne. Martin Banham's *Osborne*, in the "Writers and Critics" series, appeared in 1969, as did Alan Carter's *John Osborne*. John Russell Taylor edited the Casebook on *Look Back in Anger* in 1968. Harold Ferrar's *John Osborne*, for the "Columbia Essays on Modern Writers" series, was published in 1973 and carried critical discussion up to *Hedda Gabler*, but the next full-length work was Michael Anderson's *Anger and Detachment* in 1976, a study which he shared with Arden and Pinter. Since then Osborne criticism has been first-night notices and gobbets of gossip, and the first-night notices have grown less frequent simply because there have been fewer first nights. If we compare the attention Osborne has received with that given, say, to

Pinter, the amount seems ridiculously sparse. Now, surely, is a good time to look again at what kind of dramatist Osborne is and what he has achieved in the theater since 1956.

Arnold P. Hinchliffe

Manchester University

Acknowledgments

I should like to thank Kinley E. Roby for suggesting this volume and fostering it so amiably. For their many kindnesses I must also thank David L. Hirst, Denise Palmer, Mavis E. Pindard, Giovanni Pontiero, Patrick Procktor, Daniel Rogers and Tony Simlick. My thanks to Muriel Wayt who typed the manuscript and to Jim who was patient.

For permission to quote from the works of John Osborne I am grateful to the author and David Higham Associates, Ltd., and the following publishers:

From *Look Back in Anger,* by kind permission of Faber and Faber, Ltd., and S. G. Phillips, Incorporated.

From *The Entertainer*, by kind permission of S. G. Phillips, Incorporated.

From *Inadmissible Evidence*, by kind permission of Harold Ober Associates, Incorporated.

From *Time Present, The Hotel in Amsterdam, West of Suez* and *A Patriot for Me,* by kind permission of Dodd, Mead and Company, Incorporated.

I am also grateful for the following permissions to quote from works cited in this study:

From *Osborne* by Martin Banham, by kind permission of the author.

From *Revolutions in Modern English Drama* by Katharine J. Worth, by kind permission of the author and Bell & Hyman, Ltd.

From *Brief Chronicles* by Martin Esslin, by kind permission of the author, Curtis Brown Ltd., and Doubleday and Company, Inc.

From *Six Dramatists in Search of a Language* by Andrew Kennedy, by kind permission of the author and Cambridge University Press.

From *The Friends* by Arnold Wesker, by kind permission of the author, Jonathan Cape, Ltd., and Harper and Row, Publishers, Inc.

From *The Theatres of George Devine* by Irving Wardle, by kind permission of the author, Jonathan Cape, Ltd., and Deborah Rogers, Ltd.

From *John Osborne* by Harold Ferrar, by kind permission of the author and Columbia University Press.

From *The Language of Modern Drama* by Gareth Lloyd Evans, by kind permission of the author and J. M. Dent and Sons, Ltd.

From *Anger and After* by John Russell Taylor, by kind permission of Eyre Methuen Ltd.

From *Brecht on Theatre,* edited and translated by John Willett, by kind permission of Eyre Methuen Ltd.

From *Comedy of Manners* by David L. Hirst, by kind permission of Eyre Methuen Ltd.

From *The Modern Actor* by Michael Billington, by kind permission of Hamish Hamilton Ltd.

From *Theatre Language* by John Russell Brown. © John Russell Brown, 1972 by permission of Allen Lane, The Penguin Press and Taplinger Publishing Co., Inc.

From "The Possibility of a Poetic Drama" by T. S. Eliot, by kind permission of Methuen and Company, Ltd.

From *British Theatre since 1955: A Reassessment* by Ronald Hayman.© Oxford University Press, 1979, by permission of the Oxford University Press.

From *Anger and Detachment* by Michael Anderson, by kind permission of Pitman Books Ltd.

From *Post War British Theatre* by John Elsom, by kind permission of the author and Routledge and Kegan Paul Ltd.

From *The Writer and His Commitment* by John Mander, by kind permission of Martin Secker and Warburg Ltd., and Greenwood Press (Williamhouse-Regency Inc.).

From *The Player Kings* by Richard Findlater, by kind permission of A. P. Watt, Ltd.

Chronology

1929 Born 12 December in Fulham, London.

1941 Death of his father.

1946 Left school; worked as journalist for trade magazines such as *Gas World* and the *Miller*.

1948 "Drifted" into the theater as tutor to juvenile actors in touring group. Acted for the first time in *No Room at the Inn,* at the Empire Theater in Sheffield.

1950 May: first play (written in collaboration with Stella Linden) produced at Huddersfield.

1951 June: married Pamela Elizabeth Lane, actress.

1955 1 March: *Personal Enemy*, written with Anthony Creighton, staged at Harrogate.

1956 April: joined English Stage Company; 8 May: *Look Back in Anger*; 15 May: first appearance on London stage as Antonio in *Don Juan* and Lionel in *The Death of Satan*. Evening Standard Award as Most Promising Playwright of the Year.

1957 10 April: *The Entertainer*, directed by Tony Richardson, with Olivier in the title role. Marriage to Pamela Lane dissolved. Married Mary Ure, 8 November.

1958 *Epitaph for George Dillon* opened on 11 February. New York productions of *The Entertainer* and *Epitaph for George Dillon*.

1959 14 April: *The World of Paul Slickey* opened at the Pavilion, Bournemouth, directed by John Osborne.

1960 6 November: *A Subject of Scandal and Concern* transmitted by BBC Television. Film of *The Entertainer* released.

1961 26 June: *Luther* opened at the Theater Royal, Nottingham.

1962 19 July: *Plays for England. The Blood of the Bambergs* directed by John Dexter; *Under Plain Cover* by Jonathan Miller. *The Devil Inside Him* (written with Stella Linden in 1950) staged at Pembroke Theater, Croydon, as *Cry for Love,* by Robert Owen.

1963 Marriage to Mary Ure dissolved. New York production of *Luther*, which received the New York Drama Critics Award and the Tony Award for the Best Play of 1963. Married Penelope Gilliatt, critic and journalist, 24 May.

1964 *Inadmissible Evidence* opened on 9 September. Osborne received Film Academy's Oscar Award for screenplay of *Tom Jones*.

1965 May: directed Charles Wood's *Meals on Wheels* at Royal Court. *A Patriot for Me* staged at Royal Court, 30 June. New York productions of *Inadmissible Evidence* and *Plays for England* and stage production of *A Subject of Scandal and Concern*.

1966 6 June: *A Bond Honoured* opened at the National Theater.

1967 5 December: Penelope Gilliatt divorces Osborne.

1968 23 May: *Time Present* opened at the Royal Court followed on 3 July by *The Hotel in Amsterdam*. Married Jill Bennett.

1970 *The Right Prospectus* transmitted by BBC Television on 22 October.

1971 *Very Like a Whale* published. *West of Suez* opened at the Royal Court, 17 August.

1972 *The Gift of Friendship* published. *Hedda Gabler* opened at the Royal Court on 28 June, followed on 4 December by *A Sense of Detachment*.

1973 *The Picture of Dorian Gray* and *A Place Calling Itself Rome* published. *A Patriot for Me* revived at Watford Palace Theater.

1974 *Jill and Jack* transmitted on 11 September by Yorkshire Television.

1975 16 January: *The End of Me Old Cigar* produced at Greenwich Theater. *The Picture of Dorian Gray* produced at Greenwich Theater, 13 February. *Watch It Come Down* published.

1976 24 February: *Watch It Come Down* produced at the National Theater.

1977 Osborne divorced Jill Bennett.

1978 *You're Not Watching Me, Mummy* and *Try a Little Tenderness*, two plays for television, published. Osborne married Helen Dawson, drama critic and journalist.

1980 20 January: *You're Not Watching Me, Mummy* transmitted by Yorkshire Television. *Very Like a Whale* transmitted by ITV, 13 February.

1981 3 March: *Hedda Gabler,* abridged, transmitted by Yorkshire Television. Radio performance of *A Patriot for Me,* 15 March. *A Better Class of Person* published.

1983 *A Patriot for Me* revived at Chichester Festival Theater with Alan Bates.

Chapter One
Look Back in Anger

John James Osborne was born on 12 December 1929 in Fulham, a suburb of London. His father, Thomas Godfrey Osborne, was a commercial artist whose family came from South Wales, and his mother was Nellie Beatrice Grove. Details of his childhood and adolescence are now brilliantly recorded in the first volume of Osborne's autobiography, *A Better Class of Person* (1981). His childhood in London was dominated by a remarkable galaxy of larger-than-life relations of whom possibly only his invalid father inspired or gave affection. The lack of love comes over very strongly, as in the phrase which he uses to describe his Grandma Osborne's smile: "a thin winter of contempt." Osborne's use of quotations from the plays to illustrate his early life shows how personal material provided the basis for the plays. Thus his marriage to Pamela Lane is used for the description of Jimmy Porter's marriage to Alison, and Jimmy gets his surname from a cousin who tormented the young Osborne. Billy Rice owes much to Grandpa Grove, who was reputed to have spent a weekend in Brighton with Marie Lloyd! Osborne describes the difference between the two sides of the family—one loud, the other quiet—succinctly:

> The Osborne Row differed from the Grove Row but they had their similarities. With the Groves at Tottenham or Harbord Street the atmosphere would be violent, even physically, and thick with accumulated melodrama . . . The Osborne Family Rows, in spite of the fact that they were unheedingly Christian, were centered on the related subject of money. Their disputations were on wills, testaments, entails; who had been left out, what some loved one's real intentions had been and how subsequently thwarted after death.[1]

Osborne's father died in the early years of the war after spending many years in a sanatorium. What Osborne remembers about his childhood is that very little of it can be remembered with pleasure; but the excitement of the war remains. Most of the war was spent with his mother in London, where he attended state schools, but his father's charitable association, the National Advertising Benevolent Society, which had seen the family through the illnesses of both father and son, arranged for Osborne to go to boarding school in the west of England. Osborne was not particularly happy at school and when he was nearly sixteen he was expelled for striking the headmaster (who had switched off a radio playing Frank Sinatra). The Benevolent Society found him a job writing for trade journals such as *Gas World* and it was at this time that he bought a typewriter and started writing again. An interest in amateur dramatics led to a job as acting stage manager with a touring company and he appeared on the stage for the first time professionally as Mr. Burrells in *No Room at the Inn,* in 1948, at the Empire Theater, Sheffield. For the next eight years Osborne, medically unfit for National Service, was with stock companies in seaside resorts like Sidmouth and Ilfracombe, with a stint at Derby Playhouse. As Michael Billington points out:

> . . . it was a background of low pay, poor digs, Sunday trains and cold theaters on a Monday morning. With the establishment of so many comfortable, well-subsidized reps and the virtual disappearance of the touring network, it is hard to remember that such an era ever existed. But the meticulous observer will find much of it recaptured in early Osborne.[2]

Osborne says that he always enjoyed acting but never took himself seriously as an actor, "and neither has anyone else."[3] He married the actress Pamela Lane in 1951, and while he was living with her on a Chelsea houseboat he took the script of *Look Back in Anger* to the Royal Court Theater. They were divorced in 1957 when Osborne married Mary Ure (who played Alison in London, New York, and the film version). They were divorced in 1962 and Osborne married Penelope Gilliatt, film and later drama critic of the *Observer*, in 1963. They separated in June 1966 and Osborne did not defend the divorce action in June 1967. In 1968 he married the actress Jill Bennett (who had been cited as corespondent in the divorce proceedings) at the Chelsea Registry Office. Osborne and Jill Bennett were divorced in 1977 and in 1978 he married Helen Dawson, formerly a journalist with the *Observer*, with whom he now lives in "an Edwardian magnate's house set in 23 acres of Kent."[4]

Early Plays

Osborne claims that his first play was produced when he was seventeen and that it was "terrible." There are, apparently, several works unperformed and unpublished as well as the two plays produced outside London before *Look Back in Anger* and *Epitaph for George Dillon,* written in collaboration with Anthony Creighton and performed after *Look Back in Anger*.

Osborne showed *Resting Deep* to Stella Linden and she advised "a short sharp lesson in Pinero" and, presumably, in collaboration with Osborne provided that lesson. The play, now called *The Devil Inside Him,* was performed at Huddersfield in May 1950 (and revived at the Pembroke, Croydon, in 1962 as *Cry for Love* by Robert Owen). The play is about a Welsh youth whom the villagers think is an idiot and his family a sex-maniac because he writes poetry, but whose talents are recognized by a visiting medical student. Unfortunately a local girl tries to pass him off as the father of her child and he feels obliged to kill her. The play was directed by Patrick Desmond and the *Huddersfield Examiner* detected "real dramatic instinct" behind the play.[5]

Personal Enemy, written with Anthony Creighton, was presented by the White Rose Players at Harrogate on 1 March 1955, again directed by Patrick Desmond, and seems to be Osborne's first encounter with the Lord Chamberlain. According to John Russell Taylor it is about the response of a soldier's relative when he refuses to be repatriated from Korea, but Patrick Desmond, in a letter to the *Observer* in 1964, about problems with the Lord Chamberlain, suggests another play:

> It dealt with a McCarthy type witch hunt in Canada and the two young men accused of being "Commies" (i.e. liberals) were also smeared with the homosexual brush.[6]

However, four days before the opening night, author and director were summoned to St. James's Palace and presented with cuts that made the play "largely unintelligible." There was no time to rewrite, resubmit, or rehearse, so the play went on. It is not surprising that the *Harrogate Advertiser* (5 March 1955) found the piece uneven, though H. H. Walker, theater critic of the *Harrogate Herald*, who knew of the Lord Chamberlain's interference, thought "they very nearly succeeded in making some sense of the piece."[7]

The Royal Court Theater

When Osborne submitted his script to the Royal Court Theater and became a member of the English Stage Company he joined a family which supported him and which, more importantly, he supported to the greater good of British theater. Osborne's plays in the first five years earned the Court £50,000 as compared with the Arts Council grant of £30,000. Most of Osborne's plays written in his formative years (from 1956–72) were staged there, behind the proscenium arch, and many critics have felt this to be restrictive. Osborne has conceded that with a play like *The Entertainer* the stage at the Court was a problem (and even more so with the "epic" plays like *Luther* and *A Patriot for Me*) but he has also pointed out that he likes "to establish a kind of remoteness between the actors and the audience, which I only like to break at certain times, and I can do that in the picture-frame stage."[8] More importantly, though we can only speculate on this, there seems to have been a very close and fruitful relationship between Osborne and George Devine.[9]

The facts about the English Stage Company at the Royal Court are well known.[10] The absence of any theater for experimental work in London was strongly felt and by 1955 the English Stage Company, in its initial stages of formation, was ready to step in and fill the gap. They had very slim resources and originally intended to take over the Kingsway Theater, but in fact they moved into the Royal Court in Sloane Square, reviving memories of the great Vedrenne-Barker period at that same theater—two managements which aimed at a theater removed both by geography and purpose from the commercial aims of Shaftesbury Avenue.[11] On 2 March 1956, the first five plays were announced. The third play was *Look Back in Anger,* which would open on 8 May 1956.

If *Look Back in Anger* was not an immediate success it certainly made Osborne successful, with enough offers to keep him busy for five years, the play considered for a film, and a salary on which he had to pay his first income tax. But it was never done in the West End. Donald Albery wanted to do it but would only put it on at Wyndham's if Osborne "cut out the fun about bears and squirrels because he said it embarrassed everyone. I said 'I know it does, but I'm sorry, no.' "[12] It continues, however, to make money. In 1981 Osborne announced a video production in New York for which he got something like $50,000, which he compared to real estate: "You get a return not through more work, but through a change in values."[13]

The English Stage Company purchased first refusal rights on the next three plays (for £50) and the American rights on *Look Back in Anger* (for £200). Osborne's play, in fact, was the only one out of about 750 which the Court received in response to an advertisement in the *Stage* which the two directors, Devine and Richardson, considered.

From its opening in April 1956 ten years of continuous activity followed and, until October 1965, everything was under the direction of George Devine, who died in 1966 at the age of fifty-five. It found new writers, though it never achieved its initial hope of creating a stock company, an ensemble of actors playing together continuously. Accusations of left-wing bias in this period are simply not borne out by the list of plays produced. Whatever Devine's own political beliefs may have been, his aim at the Court was simply to give the playgoer the best available in drama. As part of its program the Court also tried to educate critics in responding to new and experimental work. Some of the momentum was lost after a while and it is fair to say that the loss of George Devine was deeply felt. But if British theater needed a movement the Court provided the impression that it had one. Foreign authors like Artaud, Brecht, and Beckett were also introduced into British theater, and most importantly—particularly for Osborne's plays—the style of acting changed:

> What it unleashed was a pride of lion-like young actors and actresses into a world of roles formerly denied to them . . . So far as the good, brave causes lamented by Jimmy Porter were concerned, there was none more swiftly won than the victory implicit in Jimmy's presence on stage.[14]

Theatrical Impact

It was this "presence" which suggested to the critic of *The Times* a comparison with Coward's *The Vortex*, "which established Mr. Coward as the sympathetic voice of another post-war generation. It has the same air of desperate sincerity . . . the heroes of both plays are neurotics, but they suffer, and when an author can convey that suffering on the stage is genuine, it matters not how thin-spirited the sufferer; we are moved."[15] It was this voice, speaking for a postwar generation, rather than the formal qualities of the play, that convinced Devine and Richardson to stage the play, and although it was immediately dubbed "kitchen-sink" and its success seemed to send the Court on a course of social realism, the initial staging was not completely naturalistic: " . . . there was a sky-cloth instead of a ceiling, and all the props were still inside the surround."[16]

Osborne himself confused the matter by describing *Look Back in Anger* as "a formal, rather old-fashioned play" that "broke out by its use of language" and confessed, in 1961, that it embarrassed him to look at it.[17] More recently he has come to think those remarks misguided:

> In fact I took a lot of daring risks. For instance, it was almost a rule when I first started working in the theater at all that you never discussed anyone on the stage who never appeared because it worried the audience . . . In *Look Back in Anger* there are about 27 people referred to and only five of them actually appear.[18]

It is easy, too, to say that *Look Back* made a lot of noise because the theater was so empty. A whole generation of playgoers had grown up who were no longer satisfied by a diet of Rattigan, T. S. Eliot, and Agatha Christie. The leading commercial production in 1956 was probably Enid Bagnold's *The Chalk Garden* at the Haymarket, with Peggy Ashcroft, Edith Evans, and Felix Aylmer. Tynan described the dialogue of this comedy as speech of "exquisite candour, building ornamental bridges of metaphor, tiptoeing across frail causeways of simile and vaulting over gorges impassable to the rational soul."[19] Osborne noted that critics had ignored Nigel Dennis's *Cards of Identity* at the Royal Court while giving serious attention to this play, which he described as "the doddering apotheosis of the English theatrical decadence of the last thirty years."[20] Yet his own play was—in one sense at least—old-fashioned. Allardyce Nicoll has pointed out that all the ingredients are similar to those used in plays between 1900 and 1930 and he makes specific comparison with *The Best People* (1926), by David Grey and Avery Hopwood, and Galsworthy's *The Fugitive* (1913).[21] Eliot and Fry, too, had been dealing with restlessness and loss of direction but in language so mannered and decorated that it was self-regarding and little else. The most immediate parallel was made by Irving Wardle, who pointed out that *Look Back* was running alongside Ronald Duncan's *Don Juan*. Both plays had heroes who were men of passion invading "the territory of good manners":

> The message is the same. England has gone to sleep behind its mask of respectability. . . . The all-important difference between the two is the language. In Duncan it is so self-admiring that it gets in the way of what was being said. . . . With Osborne you have no time to observe the stylistic pirouettes, because the sense hits you like a blow in the mouth.[22]

Clearly Osborne's early plays reflect the kind of thing he had been acting in for the last eight years and, like Pinter, he begins by writing plays which resemble them in form but which confound audience expectation either by parodying the content or abandoning it. To an older playgoer the content was shocking but to younger playgoers both situation and language were, at last, "real"—not everyone, after all, had french windows and a tennis court. *Look Back in Anger,* therefore, broke new ground even if that ground was familiar. As Ronald Duncan commented:

> The so-called "kitchen-sink" dramatists are still writing within the conventions of *Mrs. Tanqueray.* They have swopped the drama of duchesses and cucumber sandwiches for bus drivers and empty sauce bottles.[23]

In fact, though both dramatists use language differently, Osborne and Pinter are acutely aware of the cucumber sandwiches, and Osborne specifically directs our attention to them: that is part of the shock of recognition. But Osborne's hallmark, according to Wilson Knight, is his ability to rush on, expand, and exhilarate:

> The attack is delivered through an amazing resource of half-slangy, intensely modern phrases; it is a kind of poetry, coming naturally from an educated young man of low birth and blending a contumacious proletarianism with the academic tradition, for Jimmy Porter's reference is wide.[24]

Osborne has called these speeches "arias" and they are elaborate solos to be performed by a star actor. Michael Billington finds Jimmy more a typical young man in a stock company than a university graduate though Gareth Lloyd Evans sees him as using the typical language of an undergraduate—"a neutral speech" by which Osborne makes little attempt to indicate character, class, or accent:

> It is the language of educated youth feeling its feet and determined to put things right. It is the language of a certain self-conceit—often not a vicious or deep one, but a cosy one born of self-awareness of intelligence, a sense of words, and a desire to chalk up a victory in the intellectual stakes.[25]

Evans lists the characteristics of this language as eloquence, lucidity, exaggeration, repetition, and the danger of always "seeming to be on the point of breaking into a public rhetorical speech." But other critics have noted that Osborne can use silence; that his language is theatrical and hence not entirely verbal:

> . . . it is in the simple silences without movement that the sustaining energy of his characters is most nakedly revealed. Between the various and resourceful engagements of their encounters, there are moments when the characters are not fighting or defending themselves, and then they reveal their basic desires and needs, that are dumb and helpless.[26]

Such a description could almost equally apply to a play by Pinter and it hints at the Strindbergian side of *Look Back,* though initially the play was praised for what seemed like its political statement. Thus Hayman insists that Osborne does not use language to characterize Jimmy Porter; rather Jimmy is offered as a spokesman for a generation that in America would be responding to James Dean in *Rebel without a Cause* (1955):

> Without being a revolutionary, Jimmy set himself up as a pugnacious enemy of the *status quo* and of the apathy it was floating on.[27]

Jimmy, then, could be seen as a spokesman in a play with a deliberate political and social aim and, indeed, *Look Back in Anger* rapidly became, as Simon Trussler caustically remarks, "a harbinger of the New Left, of Anti-Apartheid, and of the Campaign for Nuclear Disarmament." But, Trussler also reminds us, if Jimmy's emotional needs were typical his response was clearly exceptional.[28]

Political Commitment

Jimmy Porter, obviously, would not have been clamoring to join any of these organizations but that is no answer. Coward, after watching *Look Back in Anger,* found it "electrifying" but believed "it to be composed of vitality rather than anger."[29] It is a nice distinction but we must still ask what were the roots of that vitality, the causes which made it take the direction it did take. As John Russell Taylor has pointed out, no past is "so imaginatively remote as the recent past, just out of one's own field of vision and not yet far enough away to be history."[30] Recalling the anxieties of 1956 requires a very conscious effort and even reading what contemporary observers thought was the mood of the time can be a difficult, often sardonic exercise. It was a period of labels and nouns:

> Fascism, Nazism, Communism, Spain, Imperialism, Hitler, Stalin, . . . Pearl Harbor, Hungary, Suez . . . names of violence and disaster, of guilt, betrayal, spiritual exhaustion.[31]

It was a period when Protest linked Angry Young Men in England with the Beat Generation in America—a generation responding to and finding expression about contemporary history. In England young men felt that socialism had let them down. They found that in spite of their education (which had made them rootless) the class structure still excluded them as it has excluded their ancestors for centuries; they had the privilege of a university education but they were, in Somerset Maugham's word, scum. Lumping together Osborne and Kingsley Amis or John Wain was a journalistic convenience and there is little point in exploring it here.[32] Amis's Lucky Jim has little in common with Jimmy Porter. Jim Dixon has little concern for those around him and draws back from involvement whereas Jimmy Porter cries out for people to come alive, be involved—in anything. Jimmy Porter, therefore, easily became an all-purpose hero—since he was angry about everything he embraced the angers of everyone. Most would agree with Laurence Kitchin, however, that our sympathy for him is qualified:

> He shares his home with a friend and grieves at an old woman's death. His ill-treatment of his wife can partly be condoned as the by-product of a collision of values. . . . But his job, selling sweets in a market, seems a self-imposed misuse of education, a gesture of self-pitying exhibitionism. He is less angry than petulant. . . .[33]

There is wide agreement that Osborne is not didactic. His plays are "lessons in feeling" and, therefore, "more instinctive than calculated and more passionate than coherent";[34] the social themes are not of first importance.[35] Yet for Harold Ferrar *Look Back* is

> a virtual compendium of urgent mid-century concerns; isolation and alienation, non-communication, the death of ideals and the vanishing of heroism. . . . the confrontation of nothingness, the uselessness of awareness for changing a cruel world.[36]

Ferrar, moreover, goes on to suggest that those who find this political content upsetting note Jimmy's narcissism, paranoia, sado-masochism, and escapist nostalgia and use these symptoms to discount the political content. So Jimmy, often confused with his author, is representative of a generation which is lost; a generation trying to adjust to a peacetime situation at home and confronted, internationally, with the fiasco of Suez and the spectacle of Russian tanks rolling into Hungary. Osborne's own comment on Suez is revealing:

> What made Suez a typically Tory venture was not only its deception, its distaste for the basic assumptions of democracy, but the complete ineptitude of its execution.[37]

The tone of that comment is precisely what so often foxes critics. Mander, for example, taking the hint Osborne gives us about Jimmy—"to be as vehement as he is is to be almost non-committal"—goes on to apply this to the whole play. Despite the force of Jimmy's personality and the fact that he has been taken as a spokesman for a generation Mander finds the play "fundamentally non-committal"; it does not "add up to a significant statement about anything. The anger is not realized in terms of human relationships, and worked into the dialectic of the play. . . . "[38] From this Mander pursues a familiar argument. If the play is to be taken seriously then we must take Jimmy's views seriously in their dramatic context. The play must counterpoint Jimmy against society, yet the other characters do not exist sufficiently to do this and we are left only with Jimmy's energy. The play gives us

> one powerfully realized, entirely possible human being; and a setting in which other human beings, despite the talk, are not much more than stage-furniture . . . Such values as it expresses are simply Jimmy's values, with which the author is evidently in agreement.[39]

But this, as literary criticism, will not do, either. The idea that Osborne and Jimmy are in agreement overlooks the dramatic distance the author keeps from his hero; and it can be argued that the other characters do exist, more than sufficiently. A more serious problem arises on the thematic level when a critic like Edwin Morgan takes Osborne's statement about making people feel and letting them think afterward:

> Supposing we don't make the effort—or if we do make the effort and find that no very definitely formulated theme emerges—or that a theme emerges which doesn't deserve our approbation?[40]

Osborne and Politics

Look Back in Anger was obviously not what it seemed. As Gordon Rogoff puts it:

> By what was undoubtedly an unplanned sleight-of-thought, the play gave all the appearance of being lined up with new Left political positions. It *seemed* to be about commitment, it *seemed* to be a protest, it *seemed* to be political, and it even *seemed* to be new, though the only startling "innovation" was that what *seemed* to be a five-character play was really a monologue.[41]

Now it is just possible that Osborne knew what he was doing both as a dramatist and as one concerned with politics and society. The idea that his main characters from Jimmy Porter onward speak for Osborne is seductive, and Osborne has often shown a tendency to speak like his characters—even sometimes quoting from them. It is an appealing idea since the main characters are rarely challenged within the world of the play. They do turn into public speakers but it is precisely this art of public speaking, of showmanship, that attracts Osborne. The failure of his characters to pursue a calculated and consistent program marks them out as characters and not megaphones. In 1957 Osborne was asked to make statements about his social and political beliefs but in his replies he consistently reminds us that he is an artist. Take, for example, his famous comment in "They Call It Cricket":

> I want to make people feel, to give them lessons in feeling. They can think afterwards. In some countries this could be a dangerous approach, but there seems little danger of people feeling too much—at least not in England as I am writing. I am an artist—whether or not I am a good one is beside the point now. For the first time in my life I have a chance to get on with my job, and that is what I intend to do. I shall do it in the theater and, possibly, in films.[42]

Osborne will fulfill his role as a Socialist by being an artist who cares. Thus the theater, for Osborne, is a weapon and those who work in the theater have power which they should never underestimate. The theater in which they work "must be based on care, care for how people feel and live."[43] When Osborne was sent a list of questions posed to writers by the *London Magazine* in 1957 he took care to specify that his care operated for him "as a writer working in the theater." Commenting on the indifference of writers to the problems of human freedom like Hungary and the Rosenbergs, Osborne felt these were ignored because writers find it difficult to be engaged in problems on their own doorstep. Surrounded by inertia at home it is easy to make up your mind when people are being thrown into the ash-can but now, with material prosperity, it is not easy to see that people are still being thrown into the ash-can because it is such a comfortable one. It is the writer's duty to find the language with which to speak to those people who have been thrown into the ash-can.[44] As a Socialist writer he can say very little about kinds of houses, schools, or pensions, but there are questions he can ask:

> . . . how do people live inside those houses? . . . What are the things that are important to them, that make them care, give them hope and anxiety? What kind of language do they use to one another? What is the meaning of the work they do? Where does the pain lie? What are their expectations? . . . Experiment means asking questions, and these are all questions of socialism.[45]

They are not, many critics have observed—with some justice—exactly the questions Osborne has asked in his plays. Moreover as the years have passed critics have grown uneasy as the angry rebel seemed to be turning into an irascible High Tory who would like to see "this whole hideous rush into the twentieth century halted a bit." In the Tynan interview of 1968 he was asked if he had not moved in the last few years toward a right-wing position:

> That's what people would say, but I doubt whether it's true. I've always had leftist, radical sympathies. On the other hand, I'm an authoritarian in many ways, simply because of the kind of work I do. If I didn't subscribe to some kind of discipline, I wouldn't be able to do it. In that respect, I'm inevitably a conservative rather than an anarchist. But a lot of left-wing feeling nowadays strikes me as instant-mashed-potato radicalism. It hasn't been felt through and worked through. I find it easy and superficial and tiresome.[46]

This contrasts with his backward glance from 1981 recalling the feeling—felt through and worked through—that gave rise to *Look Back in Anger*:

> . . . In the 1945 election when the Labour Party got in, people like me thought the world was going to change, but instead it became more drear

and austere. It was a dull time, joyless and timid. This was followed by the collapse of the Empire and the Suez crisis. We became very disillusioned, and out of this feeling came our writing, which so many people identified with because it was expressing what they felt themselves.[47]

Osborne, then, emerges as a serious artist concerned with social and political matters, as any dramatist must be whose work for those causes occurs in the theater; whose main weapon is language, which he uses as extrovertly when writing about socialism as he does when creating a character.

Look Back in Anger

In a review of Tennessee Williams published in the *Observer* (20 January 1957) called "Sex and Failure" Osborne suggests that a playwright criticizing another playwright is merely explaining how he would have written the plays. He could also have said that a playwright writing about another playwright tells us a great deal about himself. He praises the plays of Tennessee Williams for their portrayal of suffering and sees them as "an assault on the army of the tender-minded and tough-hearted, the emotion snobs who believe that protest is vulgar, and to be articulate is to be sorry for oneself." The plays of Tennessee Williams are about failure, which is what makes human beings interesting, and to those critics who say that the characters are neurotic and therefore *too* exceptional Osborne replies:

> Adler said somewhere that the neurotic is like the normal individual only more so. A neurotic is not less adequate than an auditorium full of "normals." Every character trait is a neurotic writ small. I like my plays writ large, and that is how these are written. . . . These plays tell us something about what is happening in America and that is something we must know about. Lacking a live culture of our own, we are drawing more heavily than ever on that of the United States . . . America is as sexually obsessed as a medieval monastery. That is what these plays are about—sex. Sex and failure.

Look Back in Anger was started in May 1955 (and, incidentally, was never called *On The Pier At Morecambe,* though some of it was written there); it is a play writ large. Its central character is a neurotic and it is about sex and failure, problems rooted in social and political history. The first thing we notice when *reading* Osborne's play is a liking for long and explicit stage directions. Osborne has since dismissed this habit of showering his scripts with "irrelevant" stage directions[48] but we cannot ignore them. They remind us of Shaw, but he at least had the excuse that his plays would not be produced and the habit of reading plays was more usual (so much so that dramatists like Ibsen published separate reading editions). Are these directions aimed at the director, the actor, the reader or, perhaps, all three? They certainly provide hints without which the text would be the poorer, like the well-known description of Jimmy:

> . . . He is a disconcerting mixture of sincerity and cheerful malice, of tenderness and freebooting cruelty; restless, importunate, full of pride, a combination which alienates the sensitive and insensitive alike. Blistering honesty, like his, makes few friends. To many he may seem sensitive to the point of vulgarity. To others, he is simply a loudmouth. To be as vehement as he is is to be almost non-committal.[49]

The location—a flat in the Midlands—and the time (early evening on an English Sunday) provide a static situation where boredom has set in and the only thing to do is talk, to pass the time. The French title, *La Paix du Dimanche,* was a good, ironic translation which also removed the need to ask what Jimmy was angry about. But the anger is important and by no means as unselective as the rambling discourse would suggest. Mention of the Sunday newspapers allows Jimmy to range over a large number of topics but they all boil down to the basic causes of Jimmy's rage: class and inertia. Sunday—always the same—emphasizes the inertia and leads into his cry for a little enthusiasm and his plea that they pretend to be human beings, alive and human. But the stage direction in the middle of this *(he bangs his breast theatrically)*[50] reminds us that this is a performance, for an audience. For when we talk of talk we mean monologue. If Jimmy is on stage the other characters are his audience and if he is not they tend to talk about him. But this is not to say that they do not *develop* as characters as many critics have suggested. In act 1 they feed Jimmy with topics of one sort or another. Alison leads to mention of her father "still casting well-fed glances back to the Edwardian twilight," which in turn leads to Jimmy and patriotism—a liking for Vaughan Williams ("Something strong, something simple, something English") and Jimmy's surprising sympathy for the Colonel. The backward glance is tempting, particularly as "it's pretty dreary living in the American Age," but Jimmy is not lost in the vision of high summer, long days in the sun, croquet and crisp linen:

What a romantic picture. Phony too, of course. It must have rained sometimes. Still, even I regret it somehow, phony or not. If you've no world of your own, it's rather pleasant to regret the passing of someone else's. I must be getting sentimental.[51]

Osborne then deflates the high seriousness with a kick at Cliff, who has been sitting there not listening. Understandably—but again lacking the kind of vitality, curiosity that characterized Madeline and that is conspicuously lacking in brother Nigel. After one brief meeting Nigel provides Jimmy with a large topic—but the speech is less about a particular Nigel and more about what Nigel stands for: all the things Jimmy hates and needs to fight. Jimmy's hatred of women is disturbing (though the comic tone qualifies the disturbance) particularly as his relationship with Cliff seems so warm. Indeed his previous relationship with Hugh was close enough to arouse the suspicions of Alison's mother, though this, again, tells us more about Alison's mother than about Jimmy and Hugh. Jimmy admits that "sometimes" he "almost" envies Gide and the Greek chorus boys, but his confession (in act 3, sc. 1) that friendship is one thing but sex is something else, and more important, puts homosexuality like nostalgia into perspective.

The noisy scenes must also be balanced with the quiet scenes. Thus, when Cliff leaves there is an interlude between Alison and Jimmy which explores the bear and squirrel relationship, the only level, fantasy, on which their marriage works. It is therefore, as Trussler suggests, compensatory rather than complementary:

Now this, surely, suggests what the play is about—or what it *was* about, before the myth-makers got to work: it explores, within a formally unexceptionable framework, a particular kind of sexual relationship, the incidental frustrations of which (expressed in Jimmy's outbursts about everything but his feelings towards his wife) just happened to set off or coincide with a theatrical chain reaction.[52]

Again, Osborne is not credited with doing what he is doing. The framework is "formally unexceptionable": Alison has just told Cliff that she is pregnant (so we know but Jimmy does not) and Jimmy describes the plot of the play by hoping that she will have a child and lose it (which she does), but his hope is that she will learn to feel:

> If only something—something would happen to you, and wake you out of your beauty sleep! . . . If you could have a child, and it would die. Let it grow, let a recognizable human face emerge from that little mass of india-rubber and wrinkles. Please—if only I could watch you face that. I wonder if you might even become a recognizable human being yourself. But I doubt it.[53]

Drawn to Alison by the relaxation her class has given her he finds that she is only a Sleeping Beauty. The causes of frustration are social and political as well as emotional. And they can be explored only if an outsider, Helena, arrives. Helena, an actress, looks as if she might fight back. Osborne's stage directions speak of the "royalty of that middle-class womanhood, which is so eminently secure in its divine rights" that she can behave with "an impressive show of strength and dignity."[54] We are also told that the strain is beginning to tell. Living with Jimmy is not easy, and though he does not know how cruel his wish for a dead child was, we do and we can appreciate that Alison needs a rest and must go away. Helena, however underdrawn, at least in act 2 ("little more than a dramatic convenience"[55]) can ask the questions that by this stage are puzzling us. Why and how did Alison marry Jimmy? Why can the marriage exist only intermittently on a nursery level—itself a fine ironic touch? This allows Alison to tell us how they met and how the image of the knight in shining armor turns into the game of bears and squirrels—"a silly symphony for people who couldn't bear the pain of being human beings any longer."[56] Helena also helps to crystallize Jimmy's feeling about feeling, which he locates as a response to death (though death is linked with virginity—about which Jimmy has been angry, too). Carter believes that this is the clue to Jimmy's anger—he cannot bear the thought of dying in the same way as his father:

> Is there not something wrong with a society which permits such a death and comfortably goes about its everyday life? Can society make people so unfeeling?[57]

But Jimmy's view of his father's death is more complex than that. His father fought in Spain and came back to die. His family were embarrassed by this, exhibiting the emotions of the middle class; his mother was only interested in "smart, fashionable" minorities and left the failure of a man with an audience of one small frightened boy who could not understand what his father was saying and could only feel despair, bitterness, the smell of death:

> You see, I learnt at an early age what it was to be angry—angry and helpless. And I can never forget it. I knew more about—love . . . betrayal . . . and death when I was ten years old than you will probably ever know in all your life.[58]

It is true that the substance of the speech is Jimmy rather than his father, and that is the point; it is a helpless Jimmy, one who fails to measure up, if through no fault of his own, to the requirements of the moment. He does not want to fail again when confronted with the death of Hugh's mum. But Helena has arranged for Alison to go home just when he needs her. Even here Osborne puts us at a distance from the emotions. His stage direction is quite specific. Jimmy cannot believe that Alison has refused him, and picking up the teddy bear he throws it downstage, where it "makes a rattling, groaning sound—as guaranteed in the advertisement."[59] Jimmy's pain at that moment is without an audience and dumb—except for that trivial comic groan.

Scene 2 introduces the Colonel and, again, stage directions indicate his character. Where his wife would have relished the situation (Alison leaving Jimmy) he is only "disturbed and bewildered by it."[60] Colonel Redfern never meets Jimmy, though, according to Jimmy, he nearly runs him down with his car. The Colonel, too, asks questions about the marriage to fill in the background. Why the sweet-stall, for example? And the sordid business of private detectives? When Alison repeats Jimmy's description of him his reply—simply and without malice—is that Jimmy has "quite a turn of phrase," which, in its modest way, is perceptive. He recognizes, too, what marriage to Jimmy has done for Alison. It has taught her a great deal though he cannot understand all this talk about challenges and revenge and cannot believe that love is really like that. His nostalgia is, like Jimmy's, more complex than critics will allow; he knows that life for him was over when he left India, though the knowledge does not alter his unhappiness. As Alison recognizes, her father is unhappy because everything is changed, and Jimmy is unhappy because everything is the same.

When Jimmy returns he is preoccupied with the death of Hugh's mum, which, characteristically, gets muddled up with Alison's not sending any flowers because Hugh's mum was "a deprived and ignorant old woman" who said the wrong things in the wrong places and could not be taken seriously. What terrifies Jimmy, of course, is that once more he has had to face death alone. When Helena slaps him he cannot even hit her back, but contact has been made and, in pain and despair, he allows her to seduce him.

Act 3 opens very much like act 1, with Helena instead of Alison at the ironing board. Circularity is much admired in Beckett but in Osborne it is criticized as primitive stagecraft. Yet, as in Beckett, things are the same but not quite. Helena, we are told in the stage directions, is looking "more attractive than before, for the setting of her face is more relaxed"[61] while Cliff has developed, too, and is "actually acquiring . . . a curiosity."[62] Though he falls into the old routine with Jimmy (this time it is Flanagan and Allen) he is preparing to leave and Jimmy provides him with the right tone to manage this: *"rather casually,"* a tone Cliff picks up in explaining that the sweet-stall is all right for Jimmy, who is educated but he needs something better. The interchange when Cliff says that his feet hurt and Jimmy advises him to try washing his socks shows the depth and easiness of their relationship but, as Jimmy admits, though Cliff has been "loyal, generous and a good friend" he is prepared to let him go for something he knows Helena will not give him, and it is this theme of women bleeding men to death, through sex, which introduces the brave-causes speech. Dying for brave causes was possible in the 1930s and 1940s but now there are no causes left. There is no longer any grand design, only the big bang, which makes death as "pointless and inglorious as stepping in front of a bus"; so all that is left for men is to let themselves be butchered by women. Again the stage direction indicates the tone: "In his familiar, semi-serious mood." Katharine Worth is perfectly correct when she points out that this speech is not meant to set us thinking about brave causes that *do* exist:

> This is not a play about brave causes but about a special kind of feeling, what Osborne has described as "the texture of ordinary despair." Jimmy is a suffering hero, and the action is designed to illuminate his suffering rather than force a conflict.[63]

But, as Alison acutely points out, Jimmy would be lost without his suffering. He may be trapped by it and lost with it but it is all he has left. Spain in a sense was the last cause about which a moral choice could confidently be made. Jimmy is quite specific—he sees himself as part of a generation that has inherited the debt of brave causes and dying for them but which is confused, understandably in the year of Hungary and Suez, about moral choices. Heroism is impossible, so all that is left is personal relationships, and for him (Alison has made it clear to her father that only some men and women talk of challenge and revenge in marriage) that experiment has failed. It is often overlooked that life without Alison is brighter and more relaxed; the tone of act 3, initially, is easy and even cheerful, but people are preparing to leave Jimmy. Cliff goes first, and then, when Alison returns, Helena too. Jimmy is described as an Eminent Victorian—"slightly comic—in a way"[64]—and the brave causes are discussed in his "familiar, semi-serious mood." Jimmy can cope with pain through language and sex. When Alison returns he avoids her challenge and they withdraw into the game of bears and squirrels on which note the play ends. As he insisted she has lost her child, she can and does grovel. She is also sterile.

This ending contains the possibility of two interpretations. The pattern is circular—we are back where we were before. In the debate after the production Tony Richardson insisted that it was a hopeful play—the relationship had improved, they were playing the game for the last time, with irony; as the stage directions suggest. Alison has really suffered, and Jimmy and she can now feel together. But for Hayman the irony does not work and the ending can only be taken as a "retreat into immature emotional cosiness."[65] Carter, feeling Alison has suffered enough, sees a reconciliation as possible:

> Alison's submission allows them to unite *hopefully* in the dream world they have created, where Alison is a gleamingly beautiful squirrel, and Jimmy a strong powerful bear, content perhaps never really to make out as successful human beings in a mundane, futile world.[66]

John Russell Taylor, who had seen the ending as escapist in *Anger and After*, is less certain in the *Casebook*:

> It seems possible that this basis of warm, animal love might, on the other side of suffering, lead to happiness, though some critics think otherwise,

and see in the ending only a temporary further escape into whimsey. Both possibilities are left open, and remarkably so in a play which has often been thought propagandist in aim.[67]

Criticism of *Look Back in Anger*

"A piece of shit" was, according to Osborne, Olivier's first reaction to the play but he was persuaded to visit it again and changed his mind. On this occasion he was accompanied by Arthur Miller, who saw *Look Back in Anger* as

> . . . the only modern, English play that I have seen. Modern in the sense that the basic attention in the play is toward the passionate idea of the man involved and of the playwright involved, and not toward the surface glitter and amusement that the situation might throw off . . . an intellectual play . . . and yet it seems to have no reflection elsewhere in the theater.[68]

As far as press reviews were concerned it is now generally agreed that the immediate reception of the play was "almost uniformly favorable" and most critics agreed that Osborne was a dramatist to watch.[69] The French reaction to *La Paix du Dimanche* was noncommittal without being vehement: "It is a play to reassure everyone: it attacks nothing, it demonstrates nothing." This seems to suggest that something was lost in translation. American audiences were intrigued as to what Jimmy was angry about:

> Jimmy "risen" from the working class is now provided with an intellect which only shows him that everything that might have justified pride in the old England—its opportunity, adventure, material well-being—has disappeared without being replaced by anything but a lackluster security. He has been promoted into a moral and social vacuum. . . .[71]

For Arthur Schlesinger, Jimmy's anger had nothing to do with either intellectual frustration or class conflict. He was angry because he would not recognize that he was a homosexual,[72] but Leslie Corina replied immediately that Jimmy was not gay and the play was about class struggles.[73] Gordon Rogoff saw him as born out of his time:

> Jimmy Porter, railing against his wife and contemporary England, was simply the old British Rajah turned inside-out, a *pukka sahib* gone sour. . . .[74]

The review that made the most impact was, of course, Kenneth Tynan's in the *Observer,* where he suggested that Osborne's picture of a certain kind of modern marriage was hilariously accurate:

> . . . he shows us two attractive young animals engaged in competitive martyrdom, each with its teeth sunk deep in the other's neck, and each reluctant to break the clinch for fear of bleeding to death. The fact that Osborne writes of this situation with charity has led many critics into believing that Osborne's sympathies are wholly with Jimmy but nothing could be more false: Jimmy is simply and abundantly alive; that rarest of dramatic phenomena, the act of original creation has taken place; and those who carp were better silent. Is Jimmy's anger justified? Why doesn't he *do* something? These questions might be relevant if the character had failed to come to life; in the presence of such evident and blazing vitality, I marvel at the pedantry that could ask them. Why don't Chekhov's people *do* something? Is the sun justified in scorching us?

Tynan found in the play qualities he had despaired of seeing on the stage—"the drift towards anarchy, the instinctive leftishness, the automatic rejection of 'official' attitudes, the surrealist sense of humor" but above all the fact that the Porters deplore the tyranny of good taste and refuse to accept "emotional" as a term of abuse. Osborne was the first spokesman for this group, a minority taste (he estimated the number in that minority at roughly 6,733,000 people), he admitted, and concluded that he could not love anyone who did not wish to see *Look Back in Anger,* the "best young play of its decade."[75]

Harold Hobson's review, if less forceful, was, in restrospect, remarkably perceptive. He detected two plays in *Look Back In Anger:*

> One of them is ordinary and noisy, and Mr. Osborne has written it with some wit but more prolixity; the other is sketched into the margin of the first, and consists of hardly words at all, but is controlled by a fine and sympathetic imagination, and is superbly played, in long passages of pain and silence, by Miss Mary Ure.[76]

This both begins to recognize the two silences with which Pinter's work has familiarized us and, more significantly, recognizes the existence of other characters in what was often called a monologue. It directs us to style and behavior as well as pain and despair. But the social questions continued to nag. This Wolverhampton Hamlet, as T. C. Worsley dubbed Jimmy, led to comparisons with *Hamlet,* brilliantly in the case of Wilson Knight,[77] casually by Mary McCarthy.[78] Hamlet, with his Oedipus complex, encouraged the psychoanalytical approach and pushed aside the social dimension of M. C. Bradbrook's comparison:

> Jimmy is a child casualty of the war before last—the Spanish Civil War. "There aren't any good brave causes any more" he says, in the year of Suez. His torrents of invective are set off by Cliff, the decent Horatio to this Hamlet of the Butler Education Act, and by the Colonel, an honest man of good will, whose Army memories are of military bands in India.[79]

This approach, according to Roy Huss, misses the point altogether. A large part of Jimmy's behavior can be explained by "the unresolved Oedipal situation in which he is enmeshed," indeed, by the classic pre-Oedipal neurosis when the child decides to turn his fear and resentment toward his mother into masochistic enjoyment. Thus all references to social iniquities are really "a subterfuge masking his underlying predicament with women" to which Osborne, "knowingly or unknowingly, gives dramatic context." Thus we cannot compare the play to Strindberg since Jimmy Porter's problem is not that women threaten him. Indeed they are propelled toward him by the same sadomasochistic impulses:

> To overlay this kind of atmosphere with a theme of social protest, as Osborne does, is to distort, not sharpen, the real dramatic focus in the play.[80]

Some might feel it was a little pretentious to analyze a character as if he were a real person. M. D. Faber defends this approach, however, claiming that it is justified "as long as we confine ourselves to the text," and so, from the "fact" that Jimmy is continually eating and drinking (and keeps a sweet-stall) we move inexorably to the conclusion that what the play really presents us with is "an orally fixated neurotic who projects his own psychological shortcomings onto the external environment."[81] Ironically, the next article, by David H. Karrfalt, is called "The Social Theme in Osborne's Plays" and opens with the sentence: "John Osborne's view of man is primarily social." The real difficulty in justifying analysis "as long as we confine ourselves to the text" is that the text is only part of the drama. Moreover, the original interpreters of Jimmy Porter—Kenneth Haigh and Richard Burton—were not the weedy neurotics the text rather invites but substantial, even heroic, figures. Jimmy is very much a mixed character—"a warm-hearted idealist raging against the evils of man and the universe" but also "a cruel and even morbid misfit in a group of reasonably normal and well-disposed people":

> In short, if Osborne intended elements of self-portrait then he did so in no uncritical mood . . . if Jimmy is offered as a "typical" hero, he is so as Hamlet is—a recognizable and recurring type, perhaps, but also a permanent possibility in the make-up of any sensitive person; but in a minority in any generation and in most individuals resolutely suppressed.[82]

This view is echoed by John Elsom, who points out that Jimmy is himself a chief example of the social malaise he attacks:

> Through Jimmy Porter, Osborne had opened up a much wider subject than rebelliousness or youthful anger, that of social alienation, the feelings of being trapped in a world of meaningless codes and customs. Osborne's ambivalence towards Jimmy is apparent even from his descriptions of him in the script. . . .[83]

When *Look Back* was revived at the Royal Court in 1968 John Russell Taylor noted that those qualities which had given it urgency and topicality thirteen years ago now seemed curiously incidental. Jimmy in this production was seen much more as a character in relation to other characters; his tirades

> . . . as something both arising out of his own nature and directed with particular purpose to those around him, to needle them out of their apathy, to stir them one way and another by challenging their social assumptions, outraging their political ideas, or even arousing them sexually by provoking them just blindly to strike out, resist, hit back.

Victor Henry, in the role of Jimmy, managed to suggest both sides of the character—the heroic Jimmy of what he says and the unheroic Jimmy of the stage directions and, though he still dominates, there was a more complete sense of the network of relationships which binds the group together:

> . . . the two women, Alison and Helena, are given a sharper and more satisfying individuality as played by Jane Asher and Caroline Mortimer respectively. Jane Asher especially manages to bring out the underlying dogged

stubbornness of Alison, the hard determination not to give in disguised under the apparent apathy. She thus makes more sense of the final bears-and-squirrels game, which now appears as a continuation and development of a complex relationship rather than a sentimental evasion of a straight admission of defeat.

This, Taylor felt, was all in the text but perhaps time was needed to remove the play from its immediate "inflammatory context" so that we could see it, and see, too, that it was the formal, old-fashioned elements that make the play "more than a spectacular flash in the pan."[84]

Pamela, in *Time Present,* warns us to listen to the content of the tone of the voice and not be trapped into taking what is said as wholly significant. Osborne himself complained very early of this inability to listen:

> At this I can hear all kinds of impatient inflections. "Well, if your characters only mean what they say some of the time, when are we supposed to know what they're getting at? What are *you* getting at? What do you *mean?*" At every performance of any of my plays, there are always some of these deluded pedants, sitting there impatiently, waiting for the plugs to come singing in during the natural breaks in the action. . . . I offer no explanations to such people. All art is organized evasion. You respond to Lear or Max Miller—or you don't. I can't teach the paralyzed to move their limbs. Shakespeare didn't describe symptoms or offer explanations. Neither did Chekhov. Neither do I.[85]

Look Back in Anger is a play full of talk, and Osborne's view of character is essentially theatrical. Jimmy has a sympathetic audience (at least on stage)—he usually knows how far he can go, though he does sometimes get carried away by the pleasure of his own images. But the interchange when Cliff breaks the news that he is leaving shows Jimmy offering Cliff the right tone to complete the break decently: the truth of what is said must be measured by the way it is said. If it is perfectly phrased it will be quite as true as any observation in civilized life should be. But is what happens in *Look Back in Anger* civilized? Again the tone helps; the play is funny. Osborne recalls that at a preview of the play a lot of students came and roared with laughter all the way through. Richardson and Devine asked in puzzlement why they were laughing and Osborne replied: because it's FUNNY. He himself thought of the play as "quite a comedy" but everybody else insisted that it was Human Drama.[86] It is foolish to take out of context certain speeches and press them for answers on causes, women, homosexuality, class, or anything else—though remarkably all the themes of the later plays are already here. Subsequently Osborne chose as his main characters men or women who had at least something of the actor in their professional life. Jimmy himself is an actor—as Michael Billington remarks:

> . . . the play plausibly reflects the problems of an actor buried in the rut of a Midland's weekly rep in the 50s, knowing that he has a talent and energy that have so far gone unrecognized.[87]

The extra turn of the screw that Osborne provides is that Jimmy does *not* know that he has talent that has gone unrecognized. The heroes that follow are also failures whose talent is questionable.

Chapter Two
The Entertainer

In his next three plays Osborne continued to survey contemporary society with pity and anger. Whereas what we remember from *Look Back* is an intensely personal cry apparently, if haphazardly, connected with social problems and political injustices, a world criticized from within the egomania of Jimmy Porter, a world so completely Jimmy that the other characters and even the plot seemed to be there simply to fulfill his expectations, in *The Entertainer* (1957) the form of the play allowed for more context and characterization. The form was an extension of Jimmy's music-hall routines into the whole play. Thus in *Look Back* we had to ask whether or not the condition of England was responsible for Jimmy; whether, as Walter Kerr remarks, a man like Jimmy would not be angry in a perfect world:

> [Jimmy] rages to no purpose he would care to discuss; he rages simply to articulate his distemper, and one feels that he would be vastly disappointed if his world ever threatened him with a promise of coherence.[1]

But if Archie Rice is an entertainer who has never really entertained, the badness of his art and performance can be related to an obviously imperfect world, to his family, his audience, and the place where he works, the music hall.

The Music Hall

In a note to the play Osborne laments that the music hall is dying and with it something of the heart of England. But he has not used music-hall techniques as a trick but rather because the music hall has its own conventions that cut across the restrictions of the naturalistic stage: its contact is "immediate, vital and direct." The note suggests Osborne's concern for England, tradition, the problems of writing plays, a people's theater, and direct communication. In his admiration for the music hall he belongs to a tradition that includes T. S.

Eliot (though he was to use the techniques only briefly in the *Sweeney* fragments):

The Elizabethan drama was aimed at a public which wanted *entertainment* of a crude sort, but would *stand* a good deal of poetry: our problem should be to take a form of entertainment, and subject it to the process which would leave it a form of art. Perhaps the music-hall comedian is the best material. I am aware that this is a dangerous suggestion to make. For every person who is likely to consider it seriously there are a dozen toymakers who would leap to tickle aesthetic society into one more quiver and giggle of art debauch. Very few treat art seriously.[2]

Is Osborne, then, only a toymaker? Peter Davison, examining Osborne's use of the music hall, suggests that the music hall he recalls began in 1848 when Charles Morton took over a pub called The Canterbury in Lambeth. In 1854 he took over an adjacent hall and made a charge for admission to what was called a music hall. Two kinds of act soon became prominent: the monologue and the cross-talk act. Davison finds the background of *The Entertainer* entirely genuine, even to the tableau of the nude Britannia:

The seedy patriotic tableau with the nude Britannia . . . is the tail end of a tradition going back one and a half centuries, a tradition aged and worn in theatrical and national life.[3]

The music-hall setting and devices clearly suited Osborne (monologue and cross-talk acts having formed the base of *Look Back*) and here they help him to break out of his room. They also make the connection between private feeling and public angers more obvious. Hobson had been correct in identifying two plays—one noisy, the other quiet—and it is now possible to recognize that the noisy play was also a kind of silence; words covering pain and suffering rather than exploring social and political problems. The connection is easier to grasp in *The Entertainer*:

The ironic, anti-heroic posture of Archie Rice, confronted with his own failure, suits Osborne better than the heroics of Jimmy Porter. Whereas Jimmy stands outside us, battering us into sensitivity (and sometimes, one suspects, *in*-sensitivity) by his verbal pyrotechnics, Archie identifies us with "the secret cause" in him. So that where audiences at *Look Back* were tempted just to stand and leave Jimmy threshing about on stage, in the final moment of

The Entertainer the whole burden of Archie's "Why Should I Care?" is shifted directly to *us*. Our contact with the play, as Osborne says of its method, is "immediate, vital and direct."[4]

Osborne has done more than use the setting as a metaphor. As most critics observed, the performance idiom is built into the play so securely that it is carried over into the domestic scenes; it is not so much a play about Archie's failure to distinguish between himself and the performer as about a man who uses performance to cope with his feelings both on and off stage. Its inadequacy in both areas is what the play is about.

One of the strands the metaphor does allow for is nostalgia. From the brief but sympathetic portrait of the Colonel and Jimmy's own semiserious backward glances in *Look Back* we now have the full portrait of Billy Rice. The past was a strong thread in the texture of *Look Back*—images applied to Jimmy (the knight in shining armor) recalled the historical hero both to condemn the present and remind us that things were really never very different. Nostalgia is a potent mood but it is an escape that Osborne and his characters recognize as unworkable. Billy's Edwardian music hall no longer exists and it can never be recalled. Osborne and his characters know this just as Jimmy can recognize the flaws as well as perpetual sunshine.

Brecht

Comparisons were also made with Brecht. The use of the music hall made the play exciting; the move between two stages—private and public—the one where events like death took place, the other where the emotions of those events had to be translated into performance—was exhilarating. Osborne had marched out of his room through the proscenium arch but was he following Bertolt Brecht? A simple answer would be no, since Osborne's theater aims at feeling (thought can come afterward) whereas Brecht, through the alienation device, aims at detached thought. But this simple answer is too simple. The third in the list of the most frequent, common, and boring misconceptions about the Epic Theater written by Brecht is that the epic theater is against emotion, and, in 1952, in the "Dialogue with Friedrich Wolf" Brecht wrote:

> It is not true, though it is sometimes suggested, that epic theater (which is not simply undramatic theater, as is also sometimes suggested) proclaims the slogan: "Reason this side, Emotion (feeling) that." It by no means re-

nounces emotion, least of all the sense of justice, the urge to freedom, and righteous anger. . . .[5]

Osborne aims at making us feel what it feels like to be Archie, a character probably based on Max Miller, with a few details taken from Tommy Trinder. But we also recognize how inappropriate his noninvolvement is in private life. Osborne's own comment in response to an entry in the *Penguin Dictionary of the Theater* by John Russell Taylor, which claimed that he had drawn "unsuccessfully" on Brecht for *The Entertainer*, was that at the time of writing the play Brecht "was little more than a name to me. I had, however, been going to the music hall before the compiler was born." And, in 1981, he recalled that it was a music-hall sketch by John Lawson called *Humanity* as remembered by his mother, not Brecht, that nudged him to the play.[6] As Osborne uses the music hall its function is very much that described by Brecht for Epic Theater, so it is not particularly helpful to suggest, as Taylor does, that Brecht's influence "is very marked in a number of incidentals" although Osborne had not grasped what Epic Theater is about. This presupposes that Osborne wished to do so. It also presupposes a view of Epic Theater that is questionable. From this Taylor goes on to suggest that realistic scenes are dropped "arbitrarily" into an "endistancing epic framework." We can, he says, only look at today by comparing it with some other era, hence nostalgia for Edwardian England which, like India in *Look Back*, becomes:

> . . . a romantic legend to be longed for as an alternative to the indecisions and false values of modern life. The intelligent political man of left-wing sympathies in Osborne tells him—and us—that it was the faults of this antediluvian world which brought our world into existence, but the incorrigible romantic looks back admiringly, and these plays are battlegrounds (hence much of the excitement) on which the two Osbornes fight it out.[7]

But Osborne has, in fact, created a three-generation play in which Billy regrets that the past is past but is very aware that it is while Jean offers some hope for the future; in between is Archie, the professional fool, caught with neither memory nor hope.

Olivier as Archie Rice

The portrayal of Archie Rice by Laurence Olivier was an obvious advantage, but with that advantage came certain dangers. Was Osborne a toymaker leaping to tickle aesthetic society into one more quiver and giggle? The part was not written *for* Olivier.[8] Devine had tempted him back to see *Look Back* again, this time in the company of Arthur Miller, and Olivier had recognized that Osborne could write vivid dialogue. He suggested that the next script should be sent to him. Osborne, who had much of his second play already written, finished it at breakneck speed only to have it rejected by the Artistic subcommittee at the Court. Devine promptly changed the members of the committee and, for good measure, demanded the right to choose plays without it. Originally Olivier wanted to play Billy Rice, but as he read the play he changed his mind. He was also keen that Vivien Leigh should play in it, though he felt that she was too beautiful, and schemes involving the wearing of rubber masks to make her look plain and ugly were considered. In the event she did not act in the play though she continued to attend rehearsals until asked not to do so. Olivier very much wanted to break out of the Establishment mold and it would be the first time in twelve to fifteen years that he would not be playing with Vivien Leigh or directing himself. With *The Entertainer* he was certainly breaking out with a vengeance. Tony Richardson, the director, was comparatively unknown, and the play was scathing about politics, the Royal Family, Suez, and patriotism and had run into the usual problems with the censor.[9] He was the first major actor to join the new wave of British Theater, reluctantly at first but later with enthusiasm. Since Archie was also Olivier's first full comedian role he prepared for it by visiting Collins Music Hall, Islington, and sitting through a variety bill that included nudes and rock-and-roll numbers. The result was brilliant:

> The surface detail of Archie Rice seemed definitive; the cheap grey suit, grey bowler and cane, bow-tie, mechanical wink, weary leer and seedy bounce; the slurred rasping voice, mixing Cockney and genteel, scraping the barrel for fake bonhomie and counterfeit randiness; the instinct for the wrong emphasis . . . But behind the gin-swilling bravado and the falsity, the actor suggested a crippling boredom and desolation. . . .[10]

With such a performance it was easy for those critics who had seen *Look Back* as a play overwhelmed by its central character to suggest that *The Entertainer* was the same, its symbolic significance lost in a one-man show. Banham complains that much of the significance is lost because of such an outstanding performance[11] while Hayman remarks that though the play was better written and constructed the rhetoric was still dependent on the actor—some of the speeches which Olivier made very moving were less so in the text;[12] which, after all, is what a text is supposed to do—provide possibilities for performance. *The Entertainer* was, however, more consciously a group play and Osborne chose it as his contribution to an anthology, *Writers' Theater,* in the hope that anyone reading it for the first time would recognize that his work does not consist of dramatic monologues! He pointed out that the performance of Brenda de Banzie as Phoebe and George Relph as Billy could hardly be described as stooges to Olivier's Archie:

> *Hamlet* without the Prince may be absurd, but no less than the Prince without *Hamlet,* who would look pretty silly carrying on as he does ("rhetoric" or "tirades" is how the critics have described it in my own plays) without Gertrude and Ophelia and all the rest. Drama rests on the dynamic that is created between characters on the stage. It must be concrete and it must be expressed, even if it is only in silence or a gesture of despair.[13]

The Entertainer

The play is dedicated to A. C. (Anthony Creighton?), who "remembers what it was like, and will not forget it." The plot is recognizably based on the Moorhouse incident during the Suez crisis; the title recalls the Scott Joplin rag (better known since *The Sting* in 1973) and it is entirely characteristic that a rather sour quotation from Kipling occurs in the text. Osborne constructs the play like a variety show, with thirteen turns on the bill and an intermission during which an advertising sheet is lowered. The location is a large seaside resort but the part that holiday makers never see, where prosperous businessmen at the turn of the century built their houses, twenty-five minutes from the front in the brougham. Osborne asks for music (the latest, loudest, and worst) and a gauze painted with enormous naked ladies and the name of the show: Rock'n Roll New'd Look. Through this gauze is the house where the Rices live—a fine house now split up into flats. Billy enters—spruce, smart, a fine figure of a man in his seventies who speaks in an Edwardian manner, "not an accent of class but of period." He also brings into the play the prejudices of that period since his first words are: "Bloody Poles and Irish!" As he settles down to read the newspaper his granddaughter Jean arrives, which allows Osborne to begin introducing characters—Phoebe, who is at the pictures, and Archie, who is at work—

and to explore Billy's dismay over the present, his backward glances to a time when women were ladies and one took off one's hat to them. Billy's nostalgia is always in terms of manners, gracious behavior, a time when women had both mystery and dignity. Later, at Mick's funeral, he recalls the time when every man wore a hat and used to raise it when passing the Cenotaph.[14] He knows his nostalgia is pointless, that the past cannot be recalled, but it does make him aware of the problems of the present. He is sorry for people living now who have never known what life was really like.

This deadness is immediately illustrated by Archie's act before the front-cloth, where his function is to fill in the spots between the nudes, and when he sings his theme song: "Why Should I Care?" Meanwhile the family continues to assemble. Phoebe returns from the pictures, where she passes the hours she is not working at Woolworth's, and the reason for Jean's sudden arrival is explained by a break-up with her financé. This was apparently caused by a disagreement over the Trafalgar Square rally but is really caused by his proposal of marriage, which she regards as the end of her attempts to make something of herself. She is an honest girl. She has worked hard trying to teach art in a youth club where she loathed the boys, but she fought them and she was getting somewhere. We also hear of her stepbrothers, Mick in the army and Frank, who refused to be conscripted and went to jail. Jean's ironic "God Save the Queen" returns us to Archie and his song about England and number one.

When Archie enters he carries into the domestic scene precisely the same desperate patter that he has used between nudes. He seems to ignore the telegram that has arrived for him (to Billy's fury) and proceeds to handle his family as if they were a rather bad audience. Osborne's stage directions make it clear that his appearance and manner are a pose assumed when he left his minor public school thirty years ago. Landladies adore him because he is a gentleman and his fellow artists call him Professor or Colonel, but he knows he belongs to no class at all and plays his part as best he can. He patronizes his family though he is wary of patronizing Jean, who he suspects is intelligent:

> Whatever he says to anyone is almost always very carefully "thrown away." Apparently absent-minded, it is a comedian's technique, it absolves him seeming committed to anyone or anything.[15]

Again, the stage directions are ambiguous but we see this technique in operation during the rest of the scene. He knows how far he can go with Billy and turns the situation when it threatens to get out of hand, and he is aware that Billy and Phoebe do not always listen to him (he complains that Phoebe tells her story over and over again, but, of course, he does the same). The family is tired and a little drunk, but it is only at the end of the act that we can understand how much of an act Archie has been putting on and why he did not need to open the telegram. He has already read the newspaper and knows that his son has been taken prisoner. Billy would have read it, too, if Jean had not arrived at the beginning of the act.

Act 2 opens with the family expecting the return of Mick. Life has taught Phoebe not to expect too much; where Billy is contemptuous of politicians she is apprehensive: expect too much and you will be disappointed. The conversation introduces Archie's successful brother, Bill, whom Phoebe admires "because he's a gentleman." Jean's response to this class distinction and Phoebe's remembrance of Bill's having helped them out of a mess and patting her arm is, essentially, right, but it also patronizes Phoebe:

> Oh, it's just that I can see brother Bill patting your arm, slipping that ten pounds in your hand, and then driving off to have dinner at his Club. That's all, Phoebe.[16]

The phrase "dinner at his Club" adds bite to her view of the scene, but it also adds prejudice—he might after all have gone home for dinner. The arrival of Archie and Frank, who is introduced as having slipped into the role of Archie's "feed," does not deflect Phoebe from her anger at Jean's comment though Archie does try (and *his* view of Bill is offhand, amiable), but it is Billy who causes the explosion by eating some of the cake Phoebe bought for Mick's return. It is all very emotional, brawling, un-British, and would embarrass Brother Bill immensely. Archie's song "Thank God I'm Normal" played before the nude Britannia (with patriotic sentiments spoken to a background of "Land of Hope and Glory") breaks the scene, and when we return the party is on a more even keel. Phoebe now raises the question of going to Canada, where her brother John has made a success of life. Archie's objection that you cannot get draught Bass in Toronto is both trivial and serious. Frank is all for leaving England. Why, he asks, should anyone stay in this cozy little corner of Europe where, if you are born with no money and no prospects, you will end up with no money or prospects? Europe, like the music hall, is a very old building—if anyone claps too hard it will fall down. As the party breaks up Jean and Archie are left, and as they talk we discover that the antagonism between Phoebe and Jean goes back to the days when Jean's mother found Archie in bed with Phoebe, walked out on him, and died. We also learn what feeling means to Archie—it is the memory of a lonely bar and a negress singing:

> . . . if ever I saw any hope or strength in the human race, it was in the face of that old fat negress . . . She was poor and lonely and oppressed like nobody you've ever known . . . but you see that old black whore singing her heart out to the whole world, you knew somehow in your heart that it didn't matter how much you kick people, the real people, how much you despise them, if they can stand up and make a pure, just natural noise like that, there's nothing wrong with them, only with everybody else.[17]

Archie has never heard anything like it since. He has heard whispers of it and he believes that Billy, years ago, heard it, but nowadays nobody feels quite like that. The alternatives are to get on with the job and do it without making a fuss, or make a fuss at a rally in Trafalgar Square. But the fuss Archie would like to make must be "the most beautiful fuss in the world" and he knows he will never do it. Will Jean? Or will she have to learn the technique, to sit on her hands rather than clap a performance? For Archie it matters little since he is dead behind the eyes before an audience as dead as he is; or so Archie would have us believe. But we listen not to what is being said but to what is being felt beneath the words. Typically, Archie has exposed himself and rallies his strength by drawing attention to something else: his proposed marriage to a young girl. When a policeman arrives he assures us, in characteristic vein, that it is only the Income Tax man who has caught up with him. When he hears the news of Mick's death, however, he moves instinctively into the blues. Critics have objected that this is a facile trick; the audience is moved because they see Archie moved, but the audience should be appalled because he responds to the event with artifice. But how else should an artist respond? With the story of the negress fresh in his and our minds Archie shapes the terrible news into an appropriate piece of art.

Osborne makes this point very clearly by opening act 3 with another blues sung by Frank. This, in contrast, is satirical, bitter, mockingly patriotic, a mood reinforced by references to what the newspapers make of the event. And Jean's attack on Archie as "two pennorth of nothing" is really only the prelude to her larger anger:

why do people allow things like this to happen to them? Is it all just for "the sake of a gloved hand waving at you from a golden coach?"[18]

Archie himself is growing desperate. The jokes about the Income Tax man and policeman on the doorstep are becoming very real and close. Billy has scotched the marriage to the young girl and his offer to perform again to get Archie out of the mess goes when Billy dies. It is at Billy's funeral that Osborne introduces us to Bill and Graham—"well dressed, assured, well educated, their emotional and imaginative capacity so limited it is practically negligible"[19]—and in a quartet we see Graham trying to persuade Jean to marry him and Bill trying to send Archie off to Canada. Archie chooses jail and Jean her own independent future:

> Here we are, we're alone in the universe, there's no God, it just seems that it all began by something as simple as sunlight striking on a piece of rock. And here we are. We've only got ourselves. Somehow, we've just got to make a go of it. *We've only ourselves.*[20]

While waiting for the police to come Archie gives his last turn, gathering the threads of the play together—the old building, the sagging Britannia, the hypocrisy, betrayal, failure—but as he puts on his hat and coat he turns, hesitates, and then breaks out of the safe relationship we have enjoyed between audience and comic:

> You've been a good audience. Very good. A very *good* audience. Let me know where you're working tomorrow night—and I'll come and see you.

Critical Response to *The Entertainer*

Kenneth Tynan was enthusiastic about Olivier's Archie Rice but then laid down in his review charges that still continue to be leveled at the play:

> When Archie is offstage, the action droops. His father is a bore and his children are ciphers: the most disquieting thing about the play is the author's failure to state the case of youth. There is a pacifist son who sings a Brechtian elegy for his dead brother, but does little else of moment. And there is Jean, Archie's daughter, a Suez baby who came of age at the Trafalgar Square Rally but seems to have lost her political ardour with the passing of that old adrenalin glow. She is vaguely anti-Queen and goes in for loose generalities . . . Rather than commit herself, Mr. Osborne has watered the girl down to a nullity, and Dorothy Tutin can do nothing with her.

> This character, coupled with Archie's wife (Brenda de Banzie, bedraggled-genteel), reinforces one's feeling that Mr. Osborne cannot yet write convincing parts for women.[21]

That Dorothy Tutin could make nothing of Jean may not be Osborne's fault—more recently she could make nothing of Shakespeare's Cleopatra. Tynan's condemnation of the other characters seems, for him, amazingly insensitive. Billy can hardly be called a bore while Phoebe is a fully drawn mental cripple who evokes sympathy as much for Archie as for herself. The three children present three points of view—Mick is killed for doing what "they" told him to do, Frank is going to emigrate, while Jean is going to fight for herself and others as she did in the Youth Club. For the living it is the deaths of Mick and Billy that act as catalyst for their decision not a political rally. Jean will almost certainly be defeated but she will at least have chosen—as does Archie—the context of her defeat.

Olivier's performance was naturally engrossing and the reviews generally looked at him (with reverence), occasionally at Brecht, frequently mentioned nostalgia (but overlooked the context of that nostalgia), and most of the time commented that the disgust and anger sounded too much like that of Jimmy Porter. Thus Brooks Atkinson praised Olivier's acting but felt the play was itself as tired as the situation it portrayed and the writing uninteresting[22] while J. C. Trewin said (in at least three places) that Olivier's performance was the only worthwhile thing in a play that was "cheaply conceived and shoddily written."[23] Ironically, when the play was revived in 1974 to open a series of Osborne plays at the Greenwich Theater, the main role was taken by Max Wall, which, as Osborne admitted, also created problems:

> The problem with Max Wall, who is a comic genius, is that people might laugh the moment he comes on. Which is what you don't want of course; you want absolute deadness.[24]

Harold Clurman explained the play's popularity by suggesting that it was a bad play—poor construction and it lacked direction—but it struck a chord with English society, which felt its sense of meaninglessness,[25] while Robert Coleman found it a tasteless disappointment.[26] Tasteless or not it captured audiences in London, though whether with love or hate was not clear, as E. Morgan wryly confessed in a letter to the *New Statesman*:

I am still not sure how we were induced to play the part written for us—to emit that deadly sound of luke-warm laughter, willing but uncertain, which gave the cue for Archie's ironic impromptu about bringing the roof down and gave point to the venom behind his surface heartiness. Pretty flat it would all have fallen if we *had* been bringing the roof down wouldn't it?[27]

It was precisely this discomfort—when the audience was denied either the total sympathy of tragedy or the detachment of comedy, when class was set against class and generation against generation—that made the play memorable. Such excitement may well be merely topical. Certainly Sheridan Morley at the revival of the play thought so:

Seen again now, so much longer after Suez, and without Sir Laurence I'm inclined to think that *The Entertainer*'s power is historical rather than for all time; seen then, it was electric and tragic and magnificent and everything the theater ought to be and almost never is.[28]

The Enduring Quality of *The Entertainer*

The Entertainer is a play about a family of three generations and as such Osborne creates in it the most complex grouping of characters until *The Hotel in Amsterdam* (1968). Jean's arrival at the beginning and the gradual assembly of the family prevent Billy from reading the newspaper all through act 1, thus holding off the news about Mick, whose imprisonment and death provide the focus for the several responses. For Billy the wogs need to be taught a lesson and Mick has gone out there to do just that, but for Frank and Jean they are the victims of Billy's world. Jean and Frank differ in their response to tragedy just as Mick and Frank had responded to the call to arms differently. Frank leaves for a better life in Canada while Jean chooses to stay and fight, rejecting the comfortable but dead world of Graham as her father rejects the comfortable world of brother Bill. Frank, having fought on the issue of conscription, has no fight left in him, while Jean, who has come alive at the Trafalgar Square Rally, works out her course of action during the play. But Archie is in the middle and survives only by technique. Carter sees the three generations as linked by a common predicament:

Billy, wearied with a life that is not what it was; Archie and Phoebe mechanically performing accepted routine; and Jean and Frank, bewildered and frustrated by their inheritance. These generations are held together not by family ties but by a common bond of predicament. The predicament that, whilst what they have at present is not much good, it is probably a lot better than anything the future will bring.[29]

It would, however, be unwise to play down the family ties. There is a great deal of feeling between these people which centers on Archie and his ability to control that feeling. Thus, though the front scenes are more shocking, more obviously social comment, they are in fact brief interludes in what is essentially a domestic play about a family in a particular situation which encouraged some critics to compare it with Chekhov or *Heartbreak House.* Shotover's shiplike house was a metaphor for England just as Archie Rice's rundown theater stands for England but, as Worth observes, Osborne aims at a different relationship with his audience. Where Shaw's characters are firmly shut behind the proscenium arch and we may identify with them or not, such freedom is not allowed in Osborne's play. The audience is compelled to act in it. We may laugh at the jokes, or not, but either way "our response is prepared for and taken into the play. The feeling of being *really* in it is uncomfortably communicated."[30]

Whether Archie is played by Olivier or not his character is more strikingly dominant than the central character in the plays after *Time Present.* We could, therefore, consider one of the strands of the play to be the role of the artist in contemporary society, the principle theme of his next play, *Epitaph for George Dillon.* With George Dillon as with Jimmy Porter the question arises about the worth of the hero—can we approve of Jimmy or George? But with Archie we have a hero who is never pathetic. He does what he can, and though he may usually have to make do with technique rather than feelings he is aware of the difference; indeed that awareness only makes his pain greater. In refusing to go to Toronto he is being neither angry nor petulant—he has been there and they do not serve draught Bass. It is characteristic that he should explain a serious reason with a light answer. He is, after all, clinging to what he has left of his integrity.

Epitaph for George Dillon

Epitaph for George Dillon was the next play by Osborne to be produced at the Court though it had been produced by the Oxford Experimental Theater Club in February 1957. It opened on 11 February 1958, directed by William Gaskill, with Robert Stephens as George.

Banham's comment that this was like a return to Scribe after the excitement of Strindberg is hardly fair since *Epitaph,* the second play written in collaboration with Anthony Creighton, is the sole survivor of five apprentice plays. The present text itself is the end-product of at least two stages of revision. Patrick Desmond had asked H. H. Walker of Harrogate to read it as they might tour it and Walker recalls that it was written in flashback style which he criticized. Walker also disliked the "anti-hero theme."[31] Critics have speculated on the parts written by Osborne and the extent of Creighton's contribution. Osborne himself says that he left

> the more tedious playmaking passages (what Stella probably called exposition) which Anthony was eager to do and concentrated on those scenes and aspects which interested me, like the entire Ruth-George scenes in the second act and Barney Evans himself. It was cobbled together haphazardly in this way in less than three weeks.[32]

As with *Look Back,* Allardyce Nicoll sees the play as a return to Edwardian and Georgian theater and finds a parallel in a farce of 1910 by R. S. Warren Bell called *Company for George.* Here, much to the disgust of her husband, a middle-aged woman brings home a young penniless aggressive intellectual.[33] Osborne's play takes place in the home of the Elliot family, "just outside London," and begins in spring and ends in winter. It is a typical suburban bourgeois home—the living room dominated by an enormous cocktail cabinet (won in a competition) and a flight of ducks painted on the wall by the son, Raymond, who was killed in the war. Mrs. Elliot, "a sincere, emotionally restrained little woman . . . who firmly believes that every cloud has a silver lining,"[34] lives there with her two daughters, Josie and Norah, a husband, Percy, and her younger sister, Ruth. She has taken a liking to a young man who has just lost his job at the office where she works and brings him home to stay. George Dillon is a young "gentleman," a vegetarian, an actor who is going to be as famous as Laurence Olivier, and a playwright. The stage directions describe him as "a walking confliction" of lethargy and passion, sincerity and dishonesty.[35]

During the war Raymond, who was also artistic (as the ducks show), had sent his mother money and Mrs. Elliot proposes to use this to keep George until he writes his play and achieves success. George's attitude is summed up when he looks at the birds and Raymond's photograph and comments: "You stupid looking bastard."

Ironically Mrs. Elliot's sister, Ruth, also has a passion for lame ducks and has just ended her experiment of keeping a promising young artist after six years. It was not that he had been promising for too long but that he had lied to her about money he had received for a review—a little success he was unwilling to share with her.

Act 2 opens with the installation of a telephone and Josie's boyfriend going off on National Service to Germany, leaving Josie free to think about George. One of Mrs. Elliot's gentleman callers arrives, allowing Osborne to discuss religion and George's "talent." Colwyn-Stuart believes in "synchronizing yourself with Providence" but George insists that only the things that can be verified are worthwhile, at which point he is asked to verify his talent. In the discussion with Ruth that follows, this "talent" is explored. Ruth herself has not only left her lover but also, after seventeen years, the Communist party, and what she has hated most during that time is "the sheer, damned bad manners of the lot of them."[36] The manners are, of course, a plea for style, integrity, and the tone of the speech has to be listened to carefully. Ruth is hurt as she was hurt when her lover returned the watch she had given him, suggesting that she could not be hurt. For a moment she and George establish rapport; she gives him the watch, he kisses her and "plays" on the cocktail cabinet as if it were a cinema organ. Ruth laughs, which she seldom does when George is funny because, as she says, she can see the "fatigue and fear in your eyes."[37] Is George any good? His reply is that he attracts hostility:

> I seem to be on heat for it. Whenever I step out on to those boards—immediately from the very first moment I show my face—I know I've got to fight almost every one of those people in the auditorium. Right from the stalls to the gallery, to the Vestal Virgins in the boxes: my God, it's a gladiatorial combat: Me against Them![38]

For George there is no such thing as failure; only waiting for success. But when Ruth insists that he might be better waiting for it outside this house George asks what she is doing in this house of caricatures who would be unbelievable on a stage. George insists that he, at least, has a mind and feelings that are all fingertips—and though artists need the Elliots of this world (and the Elliots do not need artists) Elliots have no curiosity or apprehension—there is no real laughter in them which is "the nearest we ever get, or should get, to sainthood."[39] Ruth confesses that she now lacks the courage to leave; here at least she is safe as the seasons pass; just another caricature. The question is: will George, too, dwindle into a caricature? His music-hall turn with Ruth brings them together for a brief moment and he certainly has the symptoms of talent. But has he the disease? It is, anyway, too late for Ruth, who leaves him, and he turns to a very willing Josie.

By autumn (act 3) Raymond's money has been used up and George is ill. He tries to claim National Assistance toward the rent he says he is paying, which gives Osborne an opportunity, through the Man from the Board, to ask why artists do what they do and for what (and also to make clear the deadness of the quality of life enjoyed by people like the Man from the Board). The debts are mounting up and Percy expects the police to arrive at any time. In fact the doorbell rings but it is Barney Evans, who is interested in George's play, provided that he rewrite it under the title "Telephone Tart." It is George's play that suggests how the plot will go on: getting the girl pregnant in act 3. When Ruth arrives from the doctor's to confirm that George is indeed ill and will have to go away, Josie is horrified since she is, indeed, in the family way. The second scene of act 3 is winter, when George returns to the Elliots. As he returns, Ruth leaves. Her poet is now living with a woman who publishes and is successful. George, too, has been a success and is making money. But as Ruth leaves he pronounces his own epitaph on a man who hoped he was "that mysterious, ridiculous being called an artist" but who achieved nothing, made no one happy, loved no one successfully, and was a useless bore. Even "his sentimental epitaph is probably a pastiche of someone or other, but he doesn't quite know."[40] Although Percy tries to discredit him by revealing that he is already married, that proves no barrier. His wife is a successful TV actress (and Percy is converted to George when he discovers she is his favorite actress in his favorite TV panel game!) who has not had time to divorce him and, until now, he has not had the money to divorce her. But he will; now he is home, and the family settle down to enjoy the success of their new and prosperous son, whose attitude is all too clear as he gazes once more at those bloody birds and, mechanically, breaks into a dance with his new mum, Mrs. Elliot. George has chosen success—money—and in human relationships the "warm, generous, honest-to-goodness animal" to lie at his side at night.

Obviously we look at *Epitaph* for signs of things to come—the idea that the theater is a shrine,[41] the need for curiosity (which Jimmy's Madeline had in such abundance),[42] the fear of the policeman on the doorstep which grows more real in *The Entertainer* and *Inadmissible Evidence,*[43] but, most interesting of all, perhaps, is Barney Evan's criticism of George's plays:

> Dialogue's not bad, but these great long speeches—that's a mistake. People want action, excitement. I know—*you* think you're Bernard Shaw. But where's he today? Eh? People won't listen to him. Anyway politics are out—you ought to know that.[44]

Critical Response to *Epitaph*

After the excitement generated by *Look Back* and *The Entertainer* a drawing-room comedy of the seasons, in suburbia, seems rather muted. Trussler's view—"an apprentice work unwisely resurrected—and half-heartedly revised—in its author's hour of better-deserved success"[45]—looks like a reasonable judgment. Perversely, *Epitaph* is regarded by many critics as Osborne's most satisfactory play—its anger controlled, lacking in self-pity, a restraint usually attributed to the influence of Creighton. Robert Coleman, who had found *Look Back* severely flawed[46] and *The Entertainer* boring,[47] saw *Epitaph* as a great success because of its "brilliant theatrical writing."[48] Robert Brustein, who had not been overpowered by the two previous plays, found *Epitaph* an extraordinary play superbly mounted[49] while John Russell Taylor, pointing to the play's ability "to see round the central character and offer him some genuine competition without sacrificing at all the passionate rhetorical drive of the dialogue," sees *Epitaph* as the most "wholly satisfactory of the plays Osborne has worked on."[50] Charles Marowitz, too, was enthusiastic, admiring the presentation of failure in a man who apparently crackles with talent but never makes it:

> The tragedy is not that he has become a failure, but that he has forsaken the goals for which he craved success. Such a theme, if well documented (as it is here) and well played (as it is here) can produce staggering theater, as it does here.[51]

Kenneth Tynan, however, noted that the young actor-dramatist who sponges on a family is straight out of Noel Coward's *Fumed Oak:* he behaves badly and the excuse is his genius. This play may be a clever portrait of a neurotic artist but is he a good artist or a bad one? Osborne, Tynan points out, only allows us to guess at the answer and this doubt means that the play has misfired. All three of Osborne's heroes to some extent see society as the cause of their failure, and it is important to judge whether society has wasted something valuable or not. It is no good following Worth's argument that whether George has genuine talent or not is irrelevant; he has the symptoms and these prove too much for him.[52] But the symptoms are doubtful. Tynan is correct in suggesting that *if* the play is about a mediocre writer forced to accept his mediocrity then *Epitaph* is an astounding and courageous play, particularly as it includes, as a parallel theme, the idea that contemporary society can only use third-rate talents.[53] His assimilation into the family is parallel to his assimilation into commercial art, connecting suburban values and popular entertainment.

Harold Ferrar believes that Dillon is treated ironically; he is a coward who reminds most of us of the little compromises we make. But we are never here convinced that his giving in is either a pity or a waste.[54] George E. Wellwarth is in no doubt: Dillon is simply a "lazy and basically untalented young man who is trying to become a playwright with a minimum of effort" and who finds the inertia of society too much and gives up.[55]

If there is doubt concerning what Dillon stands for there is some unanimity about the context in which his creators have placed him. Trussler compares the play to *Inadmissible Evidence,* where the shadowy nature of the other characters is skillfully suggested as part of Maitland's mental state. Here, however, the context for George is, supposedly, objective and realistic and Trussler finds it insufficient. Ruth, the only character who does answer George back, is "puzzlingly hybrid":

> Presumably, in the play's original draft, the issue of her defection from the Communist Party, and of her propensity towards lame-ducks, bulked much larger. As the play stands, however, such personality-traits remain embryonic.[56]

G. K. Hunter sums up the argument. He points out that Dillon is not the victim but the one who victimizes. His phonyness is active where that of the Elliots is passive, so his assimilation is a criticism of society's tawdry values. But the form—the rise and fall of the Artist—raises expectations that are not fulfilled:

> . . . the problems of personal relationships have been raised too insistently for us not to desire their resolution, and to the personal question about the

hero, "Do you really have any integrity?" we want more than the dusty answer it receives.[57]

The play, however, is relatively straightforward, the material is all there, and it is not even a matter of listening to the tone. When George and Ruth meet for the first time they have the feeling that they have met somewhere before; Ruth's world is collapsing—she has lost her promising artist (who fulfills his promise when she leaves him) and her political convictions. She is offered a relationship with Dillon which she refuses—even to the point of leaving the house where she has taken refuge all these years and going out into a world she hates. She is too old for casual relationships, she likes to feel safe, yet it is she who leaves while Dillon, who is young and promising, stays. But he is aware of what he is doing—though he has the excuse of T.B., he has lost Ruth, Josie is pregnant, and he is in debt—and he is terribly aware that he has come home to be a caricature among caricatures; even his epitaph is probably borrowed. The truth that Osborne wishes to force on us is that these caricatures are real; life in the suburbs is like that—evenings spent absorbed in television and days spent beneath the flying ducks. Dillon's self-pity is tinged with awareness—and his talent is used to cope with a life that he cannot face alone. His weakness is his dependence on others—his mother, then Mrs. Elliot, at times Ruth, and, at least once, Josie.

The World of Paul Slickey

According to Trussler, Osborne, harassed by the press and pigeonholed by the critics, gave vent to his frustration in a "muddled musical" while Alan Carter explains *The World of Paul Slickey* rather oddly by suggesting that Osborne left "the hostile arena of contemporary life" for musical satire.[58] The oddness is that *Paul Slickey,* after all, is a total attack on contemporary society, showing Osborne as a man of many dislikes including drama critics, the church, the peerage, advertising, censorship, pop culture, and press invasion of privacy. The step from music-hall turns in *Epitaph* and *Look Back* to music hall in *The Entertainer* to a "comedy of manners with music" must have seemed an obvious way of continuing to break out of the drawing room. Osborne's commitment to the play can be guessed at from the fact that he directed it himself. *The World of Paul Slickey* opened on 14 April 1959 at the Pavilion Theater, Bournemouth, and arrived at the Palace Theater in London in May. The music was by Christopher Whelen, the choreography by Kenneth McMillan, decor by Hugh Casson, and the role of Oakham/Slickey was played by Dennis Lotis.

Osborne dedicated it to the critics, who are variously described as donkeys, liars, self-deceivers, those who betray Osborne's England for money and some who do it for nothing. The entertainment was dedicated "to their boredom, their incomprehension, their distaste," and Osborne felt it would be "a sad error to raise a smile from them." With such a dedication the product had better be something very good indeed; unfortunately, there was very little chance that Osborne had fallen into the error of raising a smile from anyone. Apart from the multiplicity of targets—and Osborne himself undermines the main ones—the plot has a Jacobean complexity. Jack Oakham, alias Paul Slickey of the *Daily Racket,* is married to one of Lord Mortlake's daughters, Lesley, who manages a pop singer called Terry Maroon and who is having an affair with her sister Deirdre's husband, Michael, an M.P., while Jack is having an affair with Deirdre. The *Daily Racket* sends Jack down to Mortlake Hall to check whether or not Lord Mortlake has died and the family are hiding the fact to evade death duties. Lady Mortlake is trying to keep things going (not aided by a lunatic brother, George) by sponsoring Gillian, who turns out to be Lord Mortlake's natural daughter by Mrs. Giltedge-Whyte. When Lord Mortlake sees Mrs. Giltedge-Whyte he goes to bed with her and dies in the act. By the time he does die, however, death duties have been avoided but a sinister priest, Fr. Evilgreene, has persuaded him to write a will in which the money comes to him if either of the two daughters divorces her husband. Since the two couples wish to change partners a sex-change drug is introduced (allowing the theme of women seizing power to come to the fore); but Jack only pretends to take the drug, is pursued by Fr. Evilgreene, who bumps into Mrs. Giltedge-Whyte, who recognizes him as an impostor. Meanwhile Lesley has changed into a man and goes off with her sister Deirdre, Gillian gets Terry Maroon, and Jack returns to the *Daily Racket* to celebrate "that goddam bitch success."

Of the many targets the peerage comes out rather well. Lady Mort lake may be introduced in the stage directions as one "in the long tradition of magnificently gracious ninnies so familiar to English playgoers" but she emerges as something more as does her husband. Even Terry Maroon, the lift-boy turned pop singer, is decent in his limited way if he had not been manipulated by the pop industry while Paul Slickey questions his function and role:

There must be something I can do,
Something to believe,
Something better, something matters,
There's someone to grieve,
Somewhere better, somewhere finer,
There must be something I can do!
Ah, well! Who cares! Who cares!
Who the devil cares![59]

Critical Reception

This was material that Wilde or Orton could have handled—each in his own way—but not Osborne. The play received more than the usual attention from the Lord Chamberlain, who quibbled over words but permitted the sex change in the plot. Indeed, the Lord Chamberlain sent an inspector to Leeds who found no less than seven departures from the licensed text, which elicited from Osborne a dignified letter of remonstrance.[60]

The critics were invited to the opening in Bournemouth (but only, it is said, to report gossip and not to review the show) and they were given complimentary tickets for which they had to pay.[61] When the reviews did appear they were fairly hostile. As Alan Brien in *Spectator* (15 May 1959) pointed out, the play was a characteristically Osbornian gesture "that shook London's theater like a one-man earthquake," but since the play was an attack on the Establishment and particularly Establishment critics, their response was hardly surprising,[62] a theme explored by Marowitz. He suggested that the great point about *Paul Slickey* was not how badly written it was but that it provided the Establishment with a weapon to clobber the anti-Establishment movement.[63]

In fact the plots confused modern audiences and the fourteen songs were no better than those in *The Entertainer,* where they were supposed to be bad. But, above all, comedy of manners requires detachment, objectivity, which, as John Russell Taylor remarks, was hardly Osborne's way. Those passages that seemed to involve social criticism were entirely subjective—"a volley of grape-shot flying off in all directions in which the person who discharges it counts for much more than his nominal targets."[64] And those targets are handled here with customery Osborne ambivalence. Paul Slickey (the Press) emerges as a frustrated idealist while Fr. Evilgreene (the Church) is an impostor and the Mortlakes, upholders of the aristocratic situation, are amiable and sympathetic characters. The play is called *The World of Paul Slickey* but he is not sufficiently there to unify the feelings in the play. Yet the play was, as Gersh points out, perfectly timed to coincide with widespread public feeling about gossip columnists. Paul Slickey is like an episode in the life of Dillon after he had sold out (and, like Jimmy Porter and Hugh Tanner, he tries to gatecrash the homes of the rich and like them has "a charlady or something" as a mother) but here Osborne tries to treat the enemy as the central character. Hitherto the enemy—Brother Nigel or Bill—is kept off stage or barely allowed on it—but here Paul Slickey should be central. He is not, but what is worse the study of a hated social parasite turns into another self-portrait:

> The villain of the musical is not Slickey, but once again a marginal figure: the Common Man who is responsible for making journalists what they are.[65]

This isolation of the real villain, however, is important. It is a theme that runs through all the early plays and shifts much of the emphasis from the targets—Church, Royalty, and Press—though the effect of this shift is to dilute or distract rather than clarify the relationship between public apathy and the sources of power which that apathy permits to exist.

Osborne's oddest ally was George E. Wellwarth, who had dismissed *The Entertainer* as "a clumsily constructed hodge-podge" but admired *Paul Slickey* and regretted that "the intensity and frankness of the anger . . . will always prevent its being popular, for it is a good play."[66] But *Paul Slickey* is not a good play. As G. K. Hunter observes, if Paul Slickey is a development of Archie Rice and Lord Mortlake of Billy Rice and Colonel Redfern (even, in the latter case, to an Indian connection) Osborne has not been able to endow either of them with the same appreciative sympathy:

> Archie Rice's faked sentiments were "placed" for us by Archie's own knowledge of their hollowness; but Paul Slickey's dreary world of lies is deliberately left hollow, and all you can hear is the rattle. *Paul Slickey* lacks, in short, the opposition of forces which gave the other plays their depth; the enemies of self-expression are now so much in the ascendant that the only conflict left is that over the spoils.

Moreover, while the musical comedy had obvious advantages in getting over a message to a wider, less dedicated kind of audience, it has to be used with care. Comparing Osborne with Brecht or Gay, what we miss is, precisely, what the title promises, a world:

> If one is going to be as angry as Mr. Osborne one must find a target large enough to sustain it. The "world" of Paul Slickey is too small, too parochial, too monomaniac to convey the important things that Osborne has to say.[67]

So, *The World of Paul Slickey* received a fairly hostile press and, we are led to believe, fostered in Osborne "a hatred of theatrical journalism which made an attack upon critics an almost mandatory set-piece in his later plays." According to Michael Anderson, after this bitter experience he withdrew "into the comparative safety of historical material."[68] Given much of the critical response to his work his distrust of critics is perhaps understandable, but that he withdrew into the safety of historical material is surely to miss the point. He turned to historical material to give himself distance from the material, a distance that would allow him to look at contemporary society more coolly. Leaving the drawing room had proved hazardous.

Chapter Three
The Lesson of History

Osborne needed detachment and, perhaps, felt that he had written himself out as the angry young man of modern times. He turned to history for any lessons the past might provide for those modern times, looking back, but not in anger. And historical material provided him with ready-made plots and the opportunity to employ what are usually called "Brechtian" stage devices. *A Subject of Scandal and Concern* (1960) was followed by *Luther* (1961) and, later, by *A Patriot for Me* (1965).

A Subject of Scandal and Concern

This play, directed by Tony Richardson with Richard Burton as Holyoake, was transmitted by BBC TV on 6 November 1960. For a dramatist who aims to make people feel and clearly enjoys the gladiatorial conflict in the theater, television would not seem to be a very suitable medium and, from *Epitaph* onward, Osborne's view of television has hardly been complimentary. When he was reader for the Court he had the habit of marking anything he disliked as "suitable for television"[1] and in 1961 he said that what he found so boring about television was "that it *reduces* life and the human spirit." He added, also, that it was not financially very rewarding and that most of the people in charge were "dim, untalented little bigots."[2] This was, of course, written in the aftermath of trying to get his play accepted as he had written it.

The play takes the form of an illustrated lecture on George Holyoake (1817–1906), who was, so far, the last man to be imprisoned for blasphemy in England.[3] Osborne uses a Narrator, a lawyer, who promises that the audience will find nothing unfamiliar in this straightforward account of an obscure event. Although Holyoake has a speech impediment, he is an energetic lecturer for the Social Missionary Society and is to give a lecture on "Home Colonization as a means of superseding Poor Laws and Emigration" in Cheltenham, where his wife and daughter are staying with her sister. Mrs. Holyoake does not understand her husband's motives and is uncomfortable staying with her sister, who does not think it proper that Holyoake should lecture in Cheltenham and who keeps her sister and child short of food. Holyoake promises to speak to them after the lecture. It is after the lecture, however, that Holyoake, in answer to a question about the duty of man to God, observes that he cannot believe in Him. This matter is taken up very energetically by the *Cheltenham Chronicle* and Holyoake is arrested in Bristol at the end of a lecture on "Free Discussion," brought back before the magistrates, and committed to the Assizes. The act ends with the magistrates trying to persuade Holyoake to use a lawyer, but, like any Osborne hero, he insists that he is, and must remain, "alone in this matter."[4]

What emerges during the trial, however, is another Osborne theme: the press hounding an individual. It was the *Cheltenham Chronicle* that started the persecution and it is that paper which produces three witnesses from its staff to back up the charge. Holyoake's defense ranges through the right to free speech to the assertion that the accusation of blasphemy is both antiquated and an impossibility; the morality, moreover, on which it rests is based on the Old Testament, on "Thou shalt not" rather than "Thou shalt": it "has always feared the flesh and so it flees from life."[5] Because his words were only spoken he is sentenced to six months in jail.

Act 3 shows Holyoake in jail with the itch caught from his fellow prisoners. He refuses to attend prayers (reasonably enough since he does not believe in Him) or have a prison Bible. And he is quite alone. His friend had died in Bristol jail, and his daughter, too, has died and, as instructed, been buried without a minister, for which his wife cannot forgive him. Other friends have also deserted him. The Chaplain prays for grace but Holyoake cannot speak and he walks out of jail on a cold December morning with the sympathetic laughter of the Governor following him. The narrator then closes the play, as he goes off to interview another client, with words that are even more patronizing than the opening speech. Criticizing people for wanting a "solution"—"like a motto in a Christmas cracker"—he suggests that if they want a meaning they must start looking for it themselves; and if they are waiting for the commercial it is probably that they want jam on their bread, even if it is mixed with another man's blood:

That's all. You may retire now. And if a mini-car is your particular mini-dream, then dream it. When your turn comes you will be called. Good night.

Criticism of *A Subject of Scandal and Concern*

The play, as promised, is a straightforward account of the trial, in which Holyoake conducted his own defense in spite of his speech impediment and ignorance of the law, and his later experiences in prison, but it tells us little of his relationship with his wife or friends or even how he felt about the death of his daughter. The strong suggestion that the whole matter was a press conspiracy to hound Holyoake to jail may have been congenial to Osborne, but it does not absolve him from examining why the social forces lined up against him were so lined up. The narrator, John Freeman, in modern dress, tells us what is happening and brings to the play Brechtian tones and a large measure of contempt for the audience. These "Brechtian" devices may, as Taylor observes, keep us from being improperly involved in the action, but Osborne runs the risk of preventing us from being properly interested in it.[6] Holyoake himself is interesting in outline—a mild-mannered, gentle, humorous social reformer fighting a speech impediment and social injustice—but he exists only in outline. The idea that he does not know his own motives looks suspiciously here as if Osborne had not begun to consider them. Reviews were predictably split: Maurice Wiggin in the *Sunday Times* (13 November 1960) found it all "distinctly tedious," while M. Richardson in the *Observer* (13 November 1960) thought it "an exceptionally good play." Much of the discussion focused on Osborne's enthusiasm for Brecht and how far he had adopted that dramatist's techniques.

Luther

Osborne's next angry young man, like Holyoake, makes his point from the vantage of history. Paul Slickey is caught in a memorable image of smell—sour ideals underneath his emotional arm-pits;[7] Holyoake has a stammer and an itch; and Luther brings together smell and itch. The creator of such heroes can hardly be said to fear the flesh or flee from life!

Luther opened at the Theater Royal, Nottingham, on 26 June 1961. It was directed, once more, by Tony Richardson, and Albert

Finney played the part of Luther. Osborne says that the idea had been brewing a long time:

I wanted to write a play about religious experience and various other things, and this happened to be the vehicle for it. . . . I hope that it won't make any difference if you don't know anything about Luther himself and I suspect that most people don't. In fact the historical character is almost incidental. The method is Shakespeare's or almost anyone else's you can think of.[8]

The production had to wait until Finney was released from *Billy Liar*, and the Lord Chamberlain refused to license the play as it stood. When Osborne saw the list of fourteen cuts ordered by the censor he refused to accept any of them and was prepared to withdraw the play and "wait for the day when Lord Scarborough is no more." But Devine felt that this play was a big step forward for Osborne and considered turning the Court into a club, though this was against first principles and inhibited the possibility of a West End transfer. In the end, George Devine and Oscar Lewenstein went to the Palace to discuss the cuts with the Assistant Comptroller and all but four of the banned passages were restored.

Luther is divided into three acts and the twelve scenes fall into a pattern of three, six, three. The Knight, a character in 3.2, is used by Osborne to announce the place and time of each scene. The three scenes in act 1 cover Luther's admission to the Order, his life in the Order, his first Mass, and two confrontations with his father, Hans, a miner (but a miner "on his way to become a small, primitive capitalist"). As Luther takes his vows, which, freely accepted, leave the taker no longer free to disobey, Hans is both proud and resentful of his son's choice of career. He cannot understand why Martin should give up fame, fortune, and domestic bliss to become a monk, nor can we as we watch Luther in the confession scene, wracked by doubts compounded of sex, violence, and inadequacy, while his fellow monks speak of minor faults of ritual and sloth.

The second scene—Martin's first Mass—is staged symbolically: a huge butcher's knife, across it the torso of a naked man, and below it a vast cone through which Luther approaches—"haggard and steaming with sweat"—looking for "the lost body of a child, hanging on a mother's tit, and close to the warm, big body of a man."[9] Brother Weinand brings the news that Hans is attending the Mass and tries to reason with Martin, who feels that nothing has changed since his vows except that he has been taught to doubt and his bowels are clogged. Weinand points out that it is not God who is angry with Martin but rather Martin who is angry with his Father. And in scene 3, his earthly father puts forward, in the language of commerce, the plot of the play by asking whether a monk who went really bad would get his Order liquidated. Weinand answers that the Church is bigger than the individual. When Martin arrives Hans once more complains that he did not follow a worldly career with a wife and children. Martin can resist such temptations but Hans strikes a more powerful blow when he suggests that Martin only became a monk through fear—a promise in a thunderstorm—and was allowed to become a monk, again through fear, when his parents lost two sons in the plague. The act ends with Martin's cry: But what if it isn't true? Had he become a lawyer that question would hardly matter.

The six scenes of act 2 look at the world outside the monastery and the forces that Martin will oppose: authority and tradition—or, put another way, profit and power. Osborne asks that the decor for this act should be "sweeping, concerned with men in time rather than particular man in the unconscious; caricature not portraiture," and should look like a Dürer woodcut.

A brilliant performance by Tetzel selling indulgences to pay for St. Peter's in Rome is balanced by a quieter scene between Martin and von Staupitz, his Vicar General. During this scene Osborne can fill in details of Martin's success, in spite of which he remains unhappy, and von Staupitz recognizes the roots of his discontent. His obsession with the Rule is both a protection from his own instincts and a fulfillment of them; he pays exaggerated respect to the Rule to mock it and he does so because he wants to substitute "that authority with something else—yourself."[10] Characteristically this discontent erupts in a whole catalog of physical complaints. Von Staupitz knows his limitations as a man—if God will not be merciful because of the love of Christ then vows and good works will not save him. But Martin is becoming that authority he fights against; he still doubts but his power is expressed, typically, in the suggestion that if he breaks wind in Wittenberg they might smell it in Rome.

Scene 3 shows Martin arriving with his ninety-five theses at the Castle Church in Wittenberg and the opening image is a child playing who refuses Martin's hand. The preaching scene parallels that with Tetzel. Both are great movers of crowds, but where Tetzel exploits credulity and fear, Martin has only contempt for the Common

Man, who allows the Establishment to exploit that fear. His theses are in Latin but his sermon is in rough German because the people must be made to know that there is no security in "indulgences, holy busywork or anywhere in this world." This insight, typically, came to him in the privy, whereupon his bowels flushed. He takes as his text—"The unjust shall live by faith alone"—which not merely repudiates good works but emphasizes the aloneness of the good life. The fourth scene returns to a confrontation with the Church he has repudiated, in the person of Cajetan, the Church's highest representative in Germany. Cajetan is shrewd, polished, and Italian and is not prepared to listen to formal speeches or argue with Martin. He sees through Martin's pose of humility and reminds Martin that the Church is not obliged to use reason to fight rebels. But, if he were to argue with Martin, he would ask what Martin will put in place of the Church when he has destroyed it and he provides the answer:

> You're not a good old revolutionary, my son, you're just a common rebel, a very different animal. You don't fight the Pope because he's too big, but because for your needs he's not big enough.[11]

As he needs the Pope, so other people need the Church. Moreover Martin threatens the unity of Christendom: "There will come frontiers, frontiers of all kinds—between men—and there'll be no end to them."[12] The nostalgia for that mythical time of a united Europe is beautifully placed here; the faults of the Church but also its confidence and both are illustrated in the short scene that follows with Pope Leo, who risks antagonizing the Germans by excommunicating Martin. Martin's answer is to burn the Papal Bull in scene 6, where his language outdoes the vigor of Tetzel or Leo and nearly brings on another fit. Again Luther exhibits humility—he wants to be still, in peace and alone, but, as with Jimmy Porter, he would be lost if he were.

Act 3 shows Martin establishing his church and settling down to married life. The first scene takes place at the Diet of Worms and, if scenically overcrowded, it is a little thin on argument. The promised disputation with Eck is not really a disputation because the Church refuses to argue Martin out of his doubts. He has taken a vow of obedience and cannot expect to be argued into keeping it. His main argument is about his work—his writings, which he divides into three parts, all of which he justifies (to himself), but which misses, again, the point of obedience, though it establishes the faults of the Church and the nascent nationalism on which Martin rises to power. When he takes his stand he seems, for once, to be untroubled by doubt or constipation. But against this firmness of purpose we hear the music of "Ein festes Burg" and the Knight becomes a character in the action and gives us information about the Peasants' Revolt of 1524, which was speedily suppressed. Martin's protestantism had been mainly in religious terms though such terms could hardly exclude wider social and political implications. He seemed to offer freedom and a new order but his order was, precisely, what he offered. His reply to the Knight that Christians are called upon to suffer and not to fight is weak, and when he pins responsibility on God the Butcher (recalling the decor of 1.2) he is shifty. He finds strength, however, to climb *up* into the pulpit from which he can speak without interruption. His Father's ways are incomprehensible, so man is left only with faith and obedience, a message illustrated in the sermon by using the story of Abraham and Isaac (another father-son tangle). At the end of the sermon Martin moves into his game of bears and squirrels: marriage with a nun.

The last scene takes place where the play began, in the Eremite Cloister, twenty-four years after Martin joined the Order. Duke Frederick had given the monastery to Martin, who lived there with his wife and six children as well as many visitors. One of these is von Staupitz, whose presence illustrates Osborne's desire for symmetry since von Staupitz was dead in 1530. Their talk allows Osborne to sum up the consequences of Luther's disturbed bowels: his work before the Diet of Worms, his response to the Peasants' Revolt, and his creation of Germany. He has restored God to men's souls, created Germany and the German language:

> We owe so much to you. All I beg of you is not to be too violent. In spite of everything, of everything you've said and shown us, there *were* men, *some* men who did live holy lives here once. Don't—don't believe you, only you are right.[13]

Martin clutches at his abdomen and reveals that even at Worms he was not certain. He listened for God's voice but all he could hear was his own. And the ending is ambiguous too. As he plays with his son he muses that the dark may not be quite so thick but his son, too, might have dreams—or be possessed by them.

Critical Reception of *Luther*

After the rather cool nature of *A Subject of Scandal and Concern*, with its "half-hearted" use of "Brechtian" devices, the news of a second historical play was received with interest: would Osborne produce a hero who could engage our attention more directly than Holyoake? How would Osborne solve the problems of a large historical narrative? The reviews were predictably mixed. Harold Hobson was full of praise in the *Sunday Times* (30 July 1961) though rather confusingly he described the play as a Marxist view of both Catholicism and Protestantism in the *Christian Science Monitor* (15 July 1961); *The Times*, reviewing the Paris premiere, saw it as character analysis in terms of contemporary sensibility and not an historical play at all since Osborne refused to take on the wider issues (7 July 1961)—which, for Bamber Gascoigne, in the *Spectator* (4 August 1961) was its virtue:

> The play offers no analysis of the causes of the Reformation, no explanation of Luther's magnetism, not even the picture of an age. It merely shows one man's rebellion against the world into which he was born, and his search for a personal understanding of life.

Reviews suggest that, for once, an Osborne play was well received in America and Carter's explanation (this was the first play without an English background) may well be right.[14] J. Rosselli in *Reporter* (12 October 1961) found it Osborne's most coherent and well-developed play, though *Time* (30 June 1961) felt that Osborne had failed to draw his modern parallels and reduced Luther to the scatological. J. C. Trewin, too, in *Illustrated London News* (12 August 1961), felt that the play minimized a great historical figure.

Nevertheless, *Luther* restored Osborne to the position of a major contemporary dramatist and rapidly became a set-book in schools. That Osborne should write a play about religious matters should come as no surprise; from sainthood in *Epitaph for George Dillon* and church bells in *Look Back*, religion is a prevailing strand in Osborne's work. But was the result much more than, as Coward is supposed to have described it, "Pompous Hieronymous Bosch"? Kenneth Tynan, reviewing the Paris production, pointed to the obvious attractions of Luther for Osborne—a man who would defy the Pope rather than alter one word of his writings, who was hailed as a hero by the people of whose causes he thoroughly disapproved, and was dubbed "apostle of social revolution when in fact, like Luther, he preached nothing but revolutionary individualism?" Tynan also commented on the play's source, Erik H. Erikson's *Young Man Luther*, its Brechtian form—"an epic succession of tableaux conceived in the manner of *Galileo*"—and sharing with that play the topic of heresy. The language was

> urgent and sinewy, packed with images that derive from bone, blood and marrow; the prose, especially in Luther's sermons, throbs with a rhetorical zeal that has not often been heard in English historical drama since the seventeenth century.[15]

Which, since the language is often Luther's own, is hardly surprizing.

Osborne's view that the historical Luther was "almost incidental" must be kept in mind. He was chosen as a sympathetic vehicle for Osborne's own views: he has the capacity for suffering, resists authority, and has a fine turn of phrase. But how well did Osborne handle the source? The fullest treatment is by Gordon Rupp, who, with Benjamin Drewery, edited the volume on Martin Luther in the "Documents of Modern History" series published by Arnold in 1970.[16] Professor Rupp amiably discounts any expertise in discussing *Luther* as drama since he is an historian. Commenting on the vast amount of material on and by Luther, he points out that Osborne has used only one source from which the themes, all the main points, and almost all the key quotations are drawn, namely Erik H. Erikson's psychological study. He finds the numerous references to constipation damaging to the historical nature of the play—there is no evidence that Luther had troubles of this sort as a monk, or indeed before 1521 (act 3, scene 1), though after that date Luther's illnesses were many and important. But he approves of the scenes connected with the first Mass and suggests that most of the shocking things said in act 2 are authentic (though in spite of this the Catholic Church comes off somehow with dignity in the play, "which is more than can be said of Brother Martin"). He feels, however, that the play then collapses, perhaps because Erikson's *Young Man Luther* has few clues about his middle age beyond the superficial, if often repeated, charge that he let down the peasants in 1525. There are, he concludes, both fine insights and great obtuseness in the play. We are shown Luther's doubts and anguish but little of his joy or confidence: "We see the real, introverted, lonely figure, and miss his friends (he had many), and his charm. . . ."

The partiality of the portrait is not unexpected given Osborne's interest though it is surely remarkable that he can portray success as so doom-laden (an echo of George Dillon?). The isolation is to a large extent achieved at the expense of the opposition, the world which shaped him and which he shaped. Osborne's trick is deliberate, however; that world is caricature, not portraiture.

If the play proved, as Ferrar suggests, that there is more to history than case history[17] for some even the case history was not thoroughly done. Trussler complains that Luther is never seen to change nor is he shown to have the quality of changing men: he is presented as a collection of characteristics held together by one theme only, physicality, reducing him to "an anally-obsessed neurotic, who is subject to profuse sweating, chronic constipation, and epileptic fits. And who also just happened to be a religious reformer."[18]

Similarly, for Carter, too much of the action is merely reported—we are left in the air about Martin's part in the Peasants' Revolt while other things are overstressed (he notes that the same point is made in successive scenes with Tetzel, Cajetan, and Pope Leo) and any ideas that are discussed (e.g., indulgences) are discussed on a simple level while the real problem—the nature of faith—is hardly ever mentioned. We should, perhaps, recall that Osborne felt that the historical Luther was "almost incidental" and that few people knew much about him. The trouble is that a play about a historical subject tends to get in its audience people who do know about the subject.

Luther and *Galileo*

Tynan had commented on the form of the play—"an epic succession of tableaux conceived in the manner of *Galileo*" and sharing with that play the topic of heresy. Osborne himself had said that the method was Shakespeare's and he might have had *Henry V* or, better still, *Henry VIII,* in mind; he might also have saved his breath. The historical sweep of the play (or lack of it) and the ideas about society (or lack of them) naturally led to comparisons, however odious. M. C. Bradbrook described Osborne as a theatrical journalist—like George Dillon, he is ready to turn out film scripts, vehicles for actors, and, if Brecht is in fashion, a Brechtian play. Thus *Luther* "relies on Brecht's Galileo."[20] John Simon, too, claims that Osborne set out deliberately to write a genuinely English Brechtian play modeled on *Galileo* but failed, as usual, to make people, places, and issues come to life because he can only write plays about single characters.[21]

Henry Popkin insists that *Luther* is a Brechtian play and that "in some respects, Osborne's is a Brechtian hero,"though Osborne's narrow view of history imposed "upon Brecht's vast and complex dramatic scheme" is a waste of Brechtian form.[22] Trussler, quoting Brecht's definitions of epic and dramatic theater, "proves" that *Luther* cannot be epic and must be dramatic.[23] But Brecht, like Holy Writ, has a quotation for everything.

For John Russell Taylor, the play is like the curate's egg: Brechtian in parts. It is not Brechtian in the obvious sense of the English theater—there are no songs and dances and no Common Man—nor can Osborne maintain the balance, as Brecht does, between the inner forces and the outer social forces that shaped Galileo. So much time is spent on the early "psychological material" that by the time this bears fruit in rebellion and heresy and Luther

> moves out (like Galileo) into the world of repressive social forces (emanating, like those that opposed Galileo, from the Vatican), there is not much room to deal with them properly.[24]

The comparison is complex. Galileo was putting forward ideas that had been held for some time but were now politically inconvenient; Luther is concerned with a mystery—not verifiable with the best telescopes in the world. There are three scenes to six which suggest time enough and the weight of the first three is necessary to give us at least some impression of the interior torture no telescope can see. Possibly Ruby Cohn's view is more sensible; that the dramatization of his suffering only occasionally allows Luther to think of the resonances of his actions. To some extent Osborne dramatizes this through the Knight who conveys the excitement and who, when Luther refuses to accept the responsibility, smashes the banner and allows the play to close in on the doubting Luther again. This is hardly Brechtian. Osborne portrays Luther as a sublime egotist who is not concerned with what others think—who, indeed, in the last scene has to be told what he has done to the world outside himself.

The whole question of Brecht and the English stage is a vexed one. Martin Esslin suggests, in "Brecht and the English Theater,"[25] that future historians might see 1956 as the year of Brechtian influence though there was little genuine knowledge and few valid productions. The main voice was that of Tynan, who, according to Esslin, used Brecht as Shaw used Ibsen. The opening of the Royal Court coincided with the visit of the Berlin Ensemble to the Palace Theater, Cambridge Circus. This visit may not have had more than a lukewarm critical reception but it had a profound effect on the theatrical profession—affecting stage design, the use of songs, music, and so forth. Both *Luther* and *A Patriot for Me* (1965) "aim at being epic drama with a Brechtian scope and Brechtian techniques" though in *Luther* Brecht's conception was "misunderstood as a kind of lantern lecture illustrated by charades." Osborne is simply not interested in the social, cultural, and political background of the period enough to make *Luther* anything more than "an attempt to clothe personal psychological problems in the superficial garb of historical drama." This may be true. The difficulty in discussing Osborne and Brecht is that the critic has to speculate on what Osborne intended (a Brechtian play he failed to write) *and* what the word "Brechtian" actually implies. Osborne's claim that Shakespeare was his source reminds us that Brecht, too, found the open-ended nature of Shakespeare's chronicles interesting. He and Osborne may share a common source, and the form Osborne uses, finally, is sharpened by exposure to what was happening in the theater—the use of certain devices which were useful though the ends of either dramatist (if they could be fully known) would be different. Possibly the influence of Brecht on Osborne was restricted more to the subject—an historical one—than to the actual technique.

The Film of *Luther*

This is interesting because it was not made by Woodfall and the script was not by John Osborne. Filmed in 1973 for the American Film Theater, it stars Stacey Keach as Luther but otherwise draws on a strong English cast. Directed by Guy Green, the screenplay was by Edward Anhalt and is, according to the publicity, "basically faithful" to Osborne's text. There is, however, considerable rewriting, and the scene with Pope Leo is omitted. The film seems to take an oversimple view of the play and actually claims that the Knight is Luther's alter-ego.

Chapter Four

Plays for England

Although the success of *Luther* was gratifying, like its predecessor it was based for material, and even dialogue, on documentary sources, and, after the thinness of material in *Paul Slickey,* this suggested that Osborne's invention was drying up. His range of invective, however, had not.

"Letter to My Fellow Countrymen" (1961)

This was published in the same year as *Luther* and followed on from "The Epistle to the Philistines" (1960). Both are attacks on hypocrisy—social and political—and the form of both is poetic rather than polemic. Osborne said that the impulse to write the letter came from an appeal by Bertrand Russell which he found both moving and disturbing. He was moved by the spectacle of this very old man still concerned for the survival of the race and disturbed because he saw that logical and reasoned arguments would get nowhere. So he chose the form of the letter very carefully, using the method of the previous Epistle, and it was "very carefully constructed, almost like a poem," hoping that the English people would respond to this form; which they did. Unfortunately they noted that the letter was sent from France (where Osborne was living the high life he seemed to deplore) and concentrated on bits of it—like the phrase "Damn you, England"—without noticing that he had "quite carefully specified whom I meant—I meant the people who were in control of our lives. . . ."[1]

The *Plays for England* that followed took up this theme and could very well have been called *Plays Unpleasant.* Ferrar says that "the most charitable act would be to refrain from exhuming them"[2] but they represent an important step in Osborne's development though overshadowed by the play that followed. Together with *Tom Jones,* they are about an England which Osborne has always celebrated. Osborne and his heroes have not attacked the framework of society so much as those who make England weak and degenerate. Thus nostalgia and patriotism are as much part of the rebellion as satire and denunciation. Indeed, Osborne is a revolutionary rather than a rebel in the sense defined by Esther in Wesker's *The Friends:*

> My brother is a rebel because he hates the past, I'm a revolutionary because I see the past as too rich with human suffering and achievement to be dismissed.[3]

Osborne's comments on the concern which provoked the letters and, more importantly, on the care with which the form was chosen—"almost like a poem"—indicate his deepening awareness that anger must be tempered by art, or one loses one's style. Such anger is, naturally, easier to express in rhetorical outbursts (Jimmy Porter) or patter (Archie Rice) or a sermon (where one is not interrupted) but Osborne now chose fable: a double bill pointedly entitled *Plays for England,* reminiscent of Shaw, certainly, but also Wilde and Coward. There is, however, a natural resistance to the double bill in the English theater and 1962 was the first year in which the Court lost money on Osborne.

The Blood of the Bambergs

Banham dismisses this play as "not particularly funny, not particularly clever, not particularly original, and not at all effective"[4]—the lack of originality, presumably, because it recalls that old favorite Anthony Hope Hawkin's *The Prisoner of Zenda* (1894). The play was inspired (if that is the word) by the fuss surrounding the marriage of Princess Margaret and Tony Armstrong-Jones but embodies views Osborne had stated in 1957 (though Malcolm Muggeridge had shocked people by attacking royalty in the *New Statesman* in 1955). In "They Call It Cricket" Osborne had suggested that we could no longer go on laughing at the people who rule our lives; they are no longer funny—"they are murderous."[5] Recalling the complaint that one of the characters in *The Entertainer* was "vaguely anti-queen" he observed that the vagueness was entirely the result of interference by the Lord Chamberlain. He would have liked to be more explicit. People need symbols to live by, but the Church has ducked every moral issue that has been offered it and is even losing its comic value while the royalty symbol is dead: "the gold filling in a mouthful of decay."[6] Can anyone, he asked, seriously pretend that "the royal round of gracious boredom" is either politically useful or morally stimulating?

Osborne found himself distressed that there should be "so many empty minds, so many empty lives in Britain to sustain this fatuous industry" and says so in *The Blood of the Bambergs*.

Plays for England were first performed at the Royal Court on 19 July 1962. Osborne describes *The Blood of the Bambergs* as a fairy story, thus putting it in a genre and qualifying the value of the events simultaneously. It opens in a large Gothic cathedral where Paul Wimple is setting the scene on the evening before the wedding of Princess Melanie to Prince Wilhelm (or Prince Will as he is called)—the moment millions throughout the world have been waiting for. Osborne had noted, in "They Call It Cricket," that the BBC had a "staff of highly-trained palace lackeys with grave-yard voices, and a ponderous language stuffed with Shakespearian and semi-Biblical echoes"[7] and Wimple is just such a hushed commentator. Osborne's control over the tone only slips when Wimple interviews Lemon—a living craftsman (who, in fact, is in charge of the workmen who assemble the stands)—and Lemon calculates the number of schools and houses that could have been built for the cost of this wedding. The tone recovers, however, in the interview with the Minister of Culture, Ted Brown (the Archbishop cannot make the Cathedral since, like an actor for *Hamlet,* he is practicing his role for tomorrow). Brown is a recent appointment by the United Socialist party who won the recent election on the strength of promising the people a Ministry of Culture to improve this superb public service, hitherto in the hands of individuals appointed by the King. After Brown has delivered what turns out to be a party political broadcast his predecessor Colonel Taft arrives, but he is curiously unwilling to give an interview. After Wimple has departed the reason for this becomes clear. Prince Wilhelm has crashed his car into a roadblock erected to keep the whole motorway clear for his exclusive use for twenty-four hours. The problem is: what to do now. Clearly the show must go on, particularly as the King cannot last long and the obvious solution seems to be Wilhelm's brother, Prince Heinrich. Brown dismisses this possibility, pointing out to a shocked Taft that Prince Heinrich (Young Harry as he is called) is as "queer as a cucumber." Surely, Brown observes, Taft must have thought it strange that a young Prince should devote his time exclusively to the barracks and the ballet? Taft admits that he had thought going to the theater was a bit eccentric.[8] The discovery of an Australian photographer, Alan Russell, sleeping in the Cathedral offers a solution since he looks like a Bamberg; and, in fact, is one—albeit illegitimate.

Act 2 takes place in the Palace, where Russell is practicing the ritual persuaded by the news that as Prince Wilhelm he will be very wealthy. As he is eating breakfast a woman rushes in. Mrs. Robbins, married to an inspector on the buses and with three children, is an ardent worshiper of royalty and has in fact spent two days in the laundry chute for just this moment. She loves the Prince, worshiping him as God, and produces a pistol to prove it. All she wants is sex, but, as Russell points out, he must save himself for his bride. Mrs. Robbins agrees but begs a kiss and, having kissed the royal hand, shoots herself. A footman enters to remove the body but is recognized as a journalist in disguise and Colonel Taft promptly shoots him. The Princess Melanie enters and, unmoved by the corpses, looks Russell over. He warms to the idea of a Royal Wedding but she warns him that he will die of boredom as she is dying of boredom:

> My countrymen, I am so bored and most of all, I am bored with you, my people, my loyal subjects, I am so bored that even this cheap little Australian looks like relieving it for a few brief moments, now and then, in the rest of my lifetime.[9]

Yet, when Russell tries to give her the kiss she offers him, she struggles and pushes him away; she cannot bear to be touched.

The play now moves back to the Cathedral, where the wedding takes place, described in hushed tones by Wimple, commented on by a gaggle of journalists obsessed with who is wearing what and culminating in the National Anthem of the Bambergs.

The absence of a main character (even *Paul Slickey* had that) throws the weight of the play on the dramatist, who has to control the tone. Osborne is mainly successful in this but critics, once more, noted his ambivalence. Royalty is given genuine dignity and shown to be the victim of the system and the bridegroom turns out to be of the blood royal anyway. But this "ambivalence" should have directed attention to what the play was about—the illegitimate fuss. Osborne is attacking the media, the BBC, the Church, *and* the common man, who all conspire to keep this monumental sham going. His fascination for pomp and circumstance is a dramatist's natural love of show business; but he satirizes a society that is sick enough to waste Russell and Melanie in such parts.

Under Plain Cover

The second of the *Plays for England* had the accidental value of introducing Jonathan Miller to the professional theater as a director. He recalls that he had no intention of working in the theater but had just finished *Beyond the Fringe* when George Devine was looking for someone to direct a play by John Osborne which had been hawked round London and which no established director would touch. As he had six or seven weeks to spare he took it on, enjoyed the experience, and forgot about it. He never directed for the Court again.[10]

The play opens in the living room of the Turners' house in Leicester as the postman arrives with several parcels (a frequent occurrence as his conversation makes clear). Tim is half-dressed as a doctor and there is a surgical trolley as well as a couch, sheets, and blankets in the room. Since he is changing into pin-striped trousers and a black jacket his wife, Jenny, who is dressed as a housemaid, answers the bell. They have, clearly, been playing at doctors and patients and are now about to play the tea-time game. This is not "bears and squirrels" even played with irony; their attitude makes clear that they are playing roles:

TIM: Now, don't stand around here talking all day. Serve tea.
JENNY: Yes, sir.
TIM: My Lord.
JENNY: Yes, my Lord. Oh—are you a Lord?
TIM: Yes, I think so. Let's try it and see.[11]

This domestic idyll is interrupted briefly by a reporter, Stanley, who asks us to consider this ordinary couple—their hopes, fears, and little ambitions. Tim, meanwhile, has changed into boxer shorts and, with Jenny, looks at mail-order advertisements for new props and costumes which leads to a long, perhaps overlong, joke about knickers. When this begins to sag Osborne deftly turns it into the topic to be discussed by the "Critics," a BBC program that is still broadcast and still as bad as Osborne describes it. The critics see the influence of Genet (and James and Fanny Burney and, of course, Ionesco) in the knickers and as the couple settle down to play at nurse and patient, Stanley once more enters to comment on this happy ordinary couple, with two children, who are about to be parted.

A tip-off from a clerk in the local Ministry of National Insurance has revealed that they are in fact brother and sister and must, therefore, be separated. Various newspapers want the story and in rather rapid succession Jenny is whisked off to London, where she meets a young man and marries him. Tim, as a publicity stunt, is brought to the wedding. It is not clear how sickened Stanley is by the cattle-market aspect of the story though he seems to grow more and more uneasy as he arranges the wedding. At the end of the play his career as a reporter has taken a severe downward turn and he is once more outside a house in Leicester, where, he can definitely state, Tim and Jenny are living together again. His career could do with a good story and, as he says, they cannot stay hidden away for ever. As he beseeches them to come out and show themselves he collapses "drunk and miserable. Dead possibly."[12]

Kenneth Tynan devoted his review to *Under Plain Cover* and found Osborne's courage in portraying a sadomasochistic *ménage* sympathetically flabbergasting:

> We suddenly realise that this is not only a thriving affair but a genuine, working marriage; an anal-sadistic relationship need not preclude love. This is perhaps the most audacious statement ever made on the English stage.

Unfortunately "the denouement is hasty and strained."[13] Paul Slickey, disguised as Stanley, discovers that they are brother and sister, separates them for a time, and then haunts them when they have come together again. The incest exists only to allow the press to intrude. And Stanley, like Paul Slickey, is presented ambivalently, taking over the play and getting more than his share of our sympathy. The play has usually been compared, unfavorably, with Pinter's *The Lover* but they are very different, and what the comparison should bring out, as Gabriel Gersh makes clear, is that *Under Plain Cover* throws another light on Osborne's backward glances:

> When Harold Pinter treated a similar subject in *The Lover*, his props were very modern: leather, stiletto heels etc. Osborne, with great reluctance, advances as far as the age of nylon ("hard faced, unembarrassed, unwelcoming nylon"), then lets himself go on Directoire knickers and Mrs. Bloomer, and celebrates Pontings as the last stronghold of a gallant old tradition.[14]

Katharine Worth finds the connections between Osborne and Shaw fascinating. Osborne, she suggests, supplies the notes missing from the Shavian debate—those "elements that don't respond to reasonableness"—and compares *Under Plain Cover* with the odd situation sketched out between Vivie and Frank in *Mrs. Warren's Profession.* The relationship between Tim and Jenny, she points out, is established before the news is broken to them, so it is difficult to see that relationship as sensational, and if the play is weakly constructed, particularly in the scenes where Tim and Jenny are separated, it does end very strongly with the young couple together again but prisoners for nine years—as Stanley is a prisoner in the public-relations response to life although he is also trying to be a friend. It is "disturbing to think of the jokey pair who were so conscious of their luck in having all those wavelengths open to each other, being shut away or narrowed down, forced to live behind locks."[15]

The Press and Mr. Osborne

This, precisely, is the point Osborne is making. It is easy to say, with Alan Carter, that the theme of press intrusion here, as in *A Subject of Scandal and Concern*, is "his silliest and most obsessive."[16] In *Under Plain Cover*, as Charles Marowitz notes, Osborne "hammers home his anti-press sentiments like an anvil-beater playing the Light Cavalry Overture on a xylophone"[17] but Marowitz then goes on to explore the dual nature of Osborne: the Public Crusader and the dramatist of Private Lives. Osborne, Marowitz suggests, is at his best when doing the latter. What this play insists on, surely, is how difficult it is to lead a private life in present-day England. When John Freeman challenged Osborne about his attacks on the press, Osborne admitted that there had been a time when he had courted publicity but there soon came a point when the "intrusion into one's life became so intense and so unpleasant that one made every effort to avoid it." The press, Osborne believes, chooses its victims and justifies its behavior with the argument that people have a right to know about people who are in the public eye. But, in fact, like royalty, the press does not have to justify itself at all (apart from to itself, the Press Council) and both operate out of "complete moral disengagement."[18]

Tom Jones

A more cheerful note was struck by the premiere of *Tom Jones* on 26 June 1963. In 1957 Osborne said that as an artist he would do his job for socialism in the theater "and, possibly, in films"[19] while in 1961 he confessed that he enjoyed film work, which gave him the illusion of doing things, "and I find that stimulating."[20] More recently he has confessed that he hates writing films "because you're like an office boy."[21] But in 1958 Osborne, with Tony Richardson, founded Woodfall Films, the company which filmed *Look Back* (1959), *The Entertainer* (1960), both directed by Tony Richardson, and *Inadmissible Evidence* (1968), directed by Anthony Page. Osborne himself wrote the scripts for these filmed versions of his plays and for *Tom Jones*. According to John Russell Taylor, he also wrote a film script of *Moll Flanders*, unpublished and unperformed, and he admits that he has written film scripts of *The Hostage* and *The Secret Agent*—"for enormous sums of money to pay off the Inland Revenue. . . ."[22] He certainly wrote the original script for *The Charge of the Light Brigade* (1968) though in the event a script by Charles Wood was used. Looking back from 1981, Osborne regrets the break-up of Woodfall, but disagreements with Tony Richardson made it inevitable and the need for such work had passed.

Woodfall Films were responsible for films like *Saturday Night and Sunday Morning* (1960), *A Taste of Honey* (1961), and *The Knack* (1965). After this success with "kitchen-sink" films, finance for *Tom Jones* was difficult to raise, but, finally, United Artists backed it and offered distribution. It cost £500,000—one of the most expensive productions to date—but on release it proceeded to make a fortune for Woodfall Productions and win an Oscar for Osborne. It was a project directed and designed and largely acted by Court artists, the part of Tom being played by Osborne's Luther, Albert Finney.

Like Pinter with Proust, Osborne has aimed at capturing the spirit of a very large novel and published the text in 1964.[23] The dialogue is sparse though it produces memorable lines that sound like quotations from Fielding and that, in some instances, are. Osborne preserves a sense of Fielding's authorial presence (and keeps the narrative going) by using subtitles, Tom's voice over the film, and a commentator. These devices, together with technical notes, allow him the fullest range for talents previously confined to "stage directions." Through all these methods Osborne is able to combine Augustan wit and modern insights. The technical notes show Osborne (presumably?) shaping the images on the screen, as in the memorable hunt scene[24] and when he asks for a deliberate shift in the look of the film after Tom reaches London. The "subdued and natural atmosphere of the countryside" is to be replaced by the heightened colors of luxury and vice as seen through the eyes of a country boy:

> The color of the film takes on a new violence and garishness; the characters a viciousness in the world of a Rake's Progress and Gin Lane. Camera tracks down a squalid street. Every sign of violence, drunkenness, misery, debauchery.[25]

Some details have, obviously, been lost or changed. Sophia has been given more forcefulness. In Fielding she has not been abroad and though her aunt has helped with her education she remains a well-bred pastoral innocent; she certainly does not push Blifil into the canal and Osborne has conflated the nervous footpad with Partridge, who joins Jones at a very late point in the chase consequently. In Fielding, Partridge joins Jones in book 8 and the unwilling footpad tries to rob Tom after he has left St. Albans in book 12; and it is Nightingale, rescued in book 13, who introduces Tom to Mrs. Miller, whose cousin, Mr. Anderson, was the would-be robber; but the speed of a film lends urgency to Osborne's version of the rescue, the happy ending, and the final moral:

> Happy the man and happy he alone,
> He who can call today his own, he who secure within can say:
> Tomorrow do thy worst! For I have lived today.

John Dryden's translation of Horace (book 3:29) no less.

The whole film was played with a zest appreciated by most of the reviewers. Brendan Gill (*New Yorker*, 12 October 1963), Bosley Crowther (*New York Times*, 13 October 1963), Brooks Atkinson (*New York Times*, 8 November 1963), *Newsweek* (14 October 1963) and *Life* (11 October 1963) all variously praised the film and the "not-so-angry" Osborne while Derek Morgan (*Reporter* 29 [21 November 1963]) particularly singled out Osborne's able handling of the script. But Arthur Knight (*Saturday Review*, 5 October 1963) found the film unsuccessful and blamed Osborne's script while Philip Hartung (*Commonweal* 79 [25 October 1963]) felt that the film lacked the interest provided by Fielding's interventions. This overlooks Osborne's use of voices, commentator, and subtitles or, perhaps, reflects an excessive devotion to "The Man of the Hill" digression. There was, however, a general feeling that both director and scriptwriter had captured the flavor, spirit, and meaning of the original and in doing so, Osborne, once more, was charged with a retreat into nostalgia.

Yet the film confirmed not merely Osborne's awareness of style but also his belief, with Fielding, that there are worse vices than the sexual ones, that hypocrisy is the deadening factor that can deceive a character called Allworthy, who lives in Paradise Hall. Osborne himself now lives in the country, in Edenbridge, and his house is called Christmas Place! In *Tom Jones* he celebrates (and there is no other word) the values of civilized English life—the values that were endangered in the 1950s, hence the anger and despair of Jimmy Porter and Archie Rice. But he does so as another lesson from history. Looking at the novel and the movie, M. C. Battestin points out that the two must be different because Fielding was writing from a view of the orderly nature of the world while Osborne writes from a view of a disordered world.[26] This difference is to prove crucial when Osborne decides to concentrate his situations within comedy of manners. Where Fielding has an assured center from which, confidently, he can redeem his hero from vice and death and award him the woman he loves, no such center will offer Osborne a *point d'appui* in the modern world.

Chapter Five
Inadmissible Evidence

Plays for England had not been encouraging and John Russell Taylor suggested that, though it was too early to write Osborne off, it was "difficult to feel much confidence in what he will do next,"[1] an opinion that had to be revised by the 1969 edition of *Anger and After*. *Inadmissible Evidence* is arguably his finest play, looking at England in the old style—the only play to continue in a straight line from *Look Back* and *The Entertainer*. It is also the last play dominated by a large central character and it says goodbye to youth. By any standards an impressive play it will last, as Trussler says, not as myth (*Look Back*) or as a set-book (*Luther*). It was revived on 12 August 1978, directed by Osborne because, as he says, Nicol Williamson wanted him to direct the play and the Court, now taken over by "all sorts of pot and beer and Left agit-prop trogdolytes," seems to have survived the return of the two brilliant but difficult stars.[2] The first production, which opened on 9 September 1964, was not so star-studded. Tony Richardson was not available to direct the play and Osborne asked Devine to direct it, but he gave it to the incoming director, Anthony Page. It was Page who chose Nicol Williamson, who, at twenty-six, hardly seemed suitable for a part which called for a heavy-weight, middle-aged star. Williamson described Maitland in the *Saturday Review* (8 January 1966) as "a man *slipping* down the drain and desperately fighting not to do so." Osborne had hinted at the theme in previous plays—waiting for the policeman or the Tax Man—and in his interview with John Freeman in 1962: "I'm always preparing for financial disaster, and always expecting that I'm going to end up in the bankruptcy court or prison, or nobody's going to give me a job. . . ."[3]

Inadmissible Evidence

Trussler, commenting on the title, says that the play is, indeed, about the "evidence that never reaches court—the body of experience and the accumulation of disappointment which shapes but does not justify one man's motives and actions," and he remarks that the solipsistic centrality of Maitland "makes for a functioning of the minor characters which was to remain uniquely successful in Osborne's work—at least until *Hotel in Amsterdam*."[4]

The setting is "where a dream takes place." It is, in fact, Maitland's office but confused somehow with a court of law where Maitland finds himself in the dock charged with publishing "a wicked, bawdy and scandalous object" to corrupt the subjects of our Lady the Queen. Maitland pleads not guilty and hesitantly affirms his belief in the growth of technology, the need for scientists, schools, and universities, and the need to face "realistically, the issues that are important, really, central, social change, basic burning issues" which are all confused with his loss of health and his pills and the failure of his life—"tolerably bright" to begin with but, finally, "irredeemably mediocre."[5] Like Holyoake, he insists on defending himself but, unlike Holyoake, he does know about the law. Unfortunately in a dream such knowledge is useless. Mr. Jones, whom he has just dismissed as his defense counsel, now takes over the role of prosecutor, and though the prosecutor should start the court argues that Maitland has already started and should go on; which is disconcerting. Osborne uses Maitland's deposition to begin his study of the life and times of William Henry Maitland, his ex-wife, Sheila, his present wife, Anna, his mistress, Liz, sundry affairs with various women, his two children, his law office and career, and his hopes for life; the hope of friendship and love:

> I made a set at both of them in my own way. With the first with friendship, I hardly succeeded at all. No. Not at all. With the second, with love, I succeeded, I succeeded in inflicting, quite certainly inflicting, more pain than pleasure. I am not equal to any of it. But I can't escape it, I can't forget it. And I can't begin again.[6]

For, like the clients he sees during the play, the law has taken over and there is no going back from divorce, arrest, or imprisonment. At this point Maitland wakes from his dream and the actors in it begin to arrive as members of his staff, all preparing to leave the sinking ship.

Kennedy compares this opening speech with Shaw and the disillusioned rhetoric of the late plays. He points out that Shaw produces "a cadenced syntax that in itself tended to reassure or anaesthetize" but Osborne gives his disengaged man "broken syntax whose jerky rhythms create . . . at least the feeling of some yet-undiagnosed malaise."[7] For Martin Banham this opening scene is reminiscent of *The Bells*—a play Osborne was certainly familiar with from his maternal grandfather.[8] In Irving's production friends and colleagues of Mathias were the judges when he is charged with the murder of the Jewish traveler.

Maitland feels that the world is ignoring him—taxis do not see him, porters do not answer him—and he spends a great deal of time on the telephone (which incorporates monologue neatly into the dialogue). Shirley is the first to go—her excuse is pregnancy and the need to get married, but, clearly, Hudson and Jones are also preparing to leave, and as Maitland continues his harangue about the nightmare of modern life and his personal problems he seems to be collapsing. He feels he ought to be able to give a better account of himself but he finds he is not functioning properly. He wishes, sometimes, that he could go back to the beginning only he knows he would do no better if he could. Yet his sympathy for "the Bennet kid," in the Scrubs for indecent assault, suggests a wider capacity for feeling than that shown by either Hudson or Jones. True, he hardly listens to his first client, Mrs. Garnsey, but then her view of her husband is his own view of himself: "nothing really works for him."[9]

Brustein complains that act 2 "collapses into structural chaos, as the author introduces rhetorical essays on subjects only remotely related to his theme";[10] Carter suggests that act 2 is more Osborne, less Maitland. There is, he says, little point in enumerating the scenes "for they serve only as vehicles for the hero's progressive disintegration."[11] What else should they be? This is made clear by Osborne's instruction that the dream at the beginning of the play should now filter into the action though some of the action must be felt as really taking place. Thus, the telephone call which opens the act should suggest that he is speaking to someone at the other end sometimes but "sometimes it should trail off into a feeling of doubt as to whether there is anyone to speak to at all."[12] The attack on contemporary youth continues but there are fine comic comments (the description of dinner at the Watsons) and some jokes a Court audience did not expect to hear, as when he offers to buy his daughter an air cushion for the next Aldermaston March ("Save you getting felt up in Trafalgar Square too") and suggests that she is sure to marry an emergent African "if she hasn't already sent her virginity to OXFAM."[13]

The month of the play, however, saw Osborne arrested at an anti-nuclear demonstration in Trafalgar Square. Hudson will leave, and Jones; and even Mrs. Garnsey does not come back but Maitland is handed an indecency case. Maitland now sees three clients: Mrs. Tonks, played by the same actress who played Mrs. Garnsey, and Mrs. Anderson, played by the same actress who had played Garnsey and Tonks. None of this doubling took place in the film, which had other ways of showing the growing unreality of Maitland's situation, but in the theater the device works very well indeed and it is difficult not to feel, with Maitland, that unreality. Their cases concern relationships that again correspond to Maitland's predicament. As Mrs. Anderson says:

> I know I'm no good at all to him. He humiliates me, I know he hates me. I wish I could have done better. That I could go back.[14]

That one cannot go back is made clear in the interview with Maples, played (on stage) by the actor who plays Jones. His "flashes of fear are like bursts of creative energy" we are told but, like Maitland, Maples has been waiting to be arrested. Married, and with a child, he is lazy but restless, and cannot help wanting to fulfill the dream started when playing tennis at school with a boy called Shipley. His first actual sexual encounter took place, however, on a cold night, at the back of a row of shops called the something Parade, by the Midland Bank and his first brush with the police was solved by meeting that policeman three times. Finally, at Piccadilly Tube Station, what he expected to happen had happened and when it did he felt relaxed, "as if I was being loved openly and attended on" until the police put the pressure on to plead guilty. What he did was crazy but, like Maitland, Maples feels a sense of helplessness. Bill, meanwhile, knows that his daughter is waiting outside and when she enters, "cool, distressed, scared" she does not speak. But what could she say to the harangue which must seem incomprehensible to her? The young, Maitland argues, seem to have everything now; they are without guilt and full of causes and ideals and gay, touching, and stylish all at the same time:

> But there isn't much loving in any of your kindnesses, Jane, not much kindness, not even cruelty, really in any of you, not much craving for the harm of others, perhaps just a very easy, controlled sharp, I mean "sharp" pleasure in discomfiture. You're flip and offhand and if you are the unfeeling things you appear to be. . . .[15]

Liz, the impeccable mistress who has avoided any feelings of guilt, arrives, too, to say goodbye and the final moments of the play show Maitland telling his wife not to try to get in touch with him, for her own sake, as he settles down to wait for whoever comes to get him.

Trussler complains that this waiting is trapped in the metaphor of the play; the charladies would arrive before the Law Society[16] but, presumably, the Law Society would send the police, and dawn raids are not unknown. Certainly in the film version the police have been since the film opens in a prison van from which the action unfolds and to which it returns.

The Critical Response to *Inadmissible Evidence*

It had become, through repetition, a universally acknowledged truth that Osborne could not handle other characters and there was, for once, some agreement that he had solved that problem in this play. He might even be said to have spelled out, in capital letters, that one of his main themes was that nobody listened, nobody connected, and that this drives a man mad. Maitland finds himself in a world conspiring to ignore his existence, a world that he finds detestable; thus the play balances the suffering hero and the context of social criticism. Here is a man, twice married, with two overprivileged children, a mistress, frequent sexual encounters, struggling to keep his business afloat who has lost

> that little adjustment mechanism for survival that keeps everyone else going and he can no longer kid himself that his work is a humane contribution to a technology-engulfed society he despises, or that the law can make provision for human complexity and suffering, or that his relationships are fulfilling.[17]

But Maitland's suffering is something deeper than a lost spring; he has, like all Osborne heroes, that special temperament that is so disturbing. He keeps the problems of others in mind—he has time for Bennet when no one else has—even while he is sinking beneath the perception of his own; and he damns himself. As Walter Kerr points out, society and the times have left him free; he makes a career of borrowing other men's work, accepts no responsibility for his children, and there are no limitations such as social or religious forces could impose on his sexual activities:

Since he has not been called guilty of anything specific, he now feels himself guilty of everything generally. He most literally despises himself, and . . . he spends his every waking hour teaching others to detest him.[18]

This feeling renders him impotent and Laurence Kitchin sees it as puritanical and very English:

If you sum up Maitland as an object of scandal and concern, the scandal—at a small-time office level—is uniformly vigorous and witty. The concern is inflated and sentimental . . . The man we have been spending all this time with is irreverent, witty and abundantly virile. For this he is punished by a prolonged hand-out of the wages of sin. How very provincial, how very puritanical . . . how very English.[19]

It is also, perhaps, very Osborne, which ensured the presence of dissenting voices. Robert Brustein, for example, feels that the solipsism threatened in previous plays reaches its ultimate here. Other characters appear only to stimulate Maitland's anger or disgust and they are "as cardboard as the scenery and sometimes just as mute" while Osborne introduces "editorials" on a variety of topics which are not merely largely irrelevant but which also go almost wholly unchallenged. The form of the play is botched and unified only by its central character. The opening scene is out of key with the rest of the production, which is realistic, though, he concedes, that realism is broken occasionally by inapposite devices and he concludes that Osborne still cannot write a coherent play but continues to create magnificent roles.[20] This, in a play where the character is the form, is a distinction too nice to be useful.

A Patriot for Me

There are few of Osborne's plays from *Personal Enemy* onward that do not have some reference to homosexuality—indeed it has been argued that the guilt felt by some of the characters stemmed from unaccepted homosexuality. But this is the first play in which the central character is a homosexual. The Lord Chamberlain had been permissive about the homosexual scenes in *Inadmissible Evidence*, but in 1964 the Assistant Comptroller warned the Royal Court that there were whole scenes in *A Patriot for Me* which could not be licensed "on the grounds that they exploit homosexuality in a manner that may tend to have corrupting influences." The ball scene, for example, would not be permitted, though the Lord Chamberlain acknowledged the merits of the piece. The cuts ordered were, this time, so damaging that the only way the play could be performed was by turning the Court into a Club, thus departing from its first principle, that the company should conduct its experiments in the presence of the general public. The play was unsuitable for performance at the Court if it could not be staged elsewhere; it was better suited to somewhere like Drury Lane! It has twenty-three mainly naturalistic scenes and about eighty-seven characters requiring at least thirty-seven actors and four musicians, all in costume. The run had to be limited to just over six weeks, so, although it played to 94 percent financial capacity, it lost over £15,000 (of which Osborne personally bore half). It could not transfer to another theater because of the ban and was not revived anywhere until 1973—at Watford Palace Theatre. It was performed at the Chichester Institute Theatre in 1983.

There was also the problem of finding about forty actors who were not afraid of being associated with a play like this. Originally planned for April, the production had to be postponed until the role of Redl was filled (the part was finally accepted by Maximilian Schell). Baron von Epp was written for George Devine, who liked it and was available, but the director, Anthony Page, was not disposed to accept this arrangement and offered it to some thirty actors (including Noel Coward, John Gielgud, and Micheál Macliammóir) who refused it and so it returned to Devine. He was still asked to audition for the part—he refused. The play was awarded the *Evening Standard* prize for the Best Play of 1965 and while it was running the Court submitted another play to the Lord Chamberlain. It was called *Saved*, by Edward Bond.[21]

The source of the play appears to have been a report in *The Times* (30 May 1913), "Suicide of an Austrian Officer," used as a background for act 3, scene 9, though, of course, there had been the John Vassall scandal in 1962. Vassall, a homosexual civil servant with access to confidential material, had been blackmailed by the Russians into copying documents for them. It was even possible that the Russians themselves betrayed him to the British government because the scandal, following on the Burgess-Maclean defection in 1951, would do more harm than any information Vassall could pass on. In 1963 Kim Philby, too, fled to Moscow though that year also saw the Profumo affair, which suggested that heterosexuals had problems too. The title comes from a remark by Emperor Franz III, who, discussing the promotion of a junior officer, was told that he was a patriot. The

Emperor replied: Ah! but is he a patriot for me? Osborne takes the career of a hard-working, able, but working-class officer (who happens to be a Jew and a homosexual) and relates it to the society in which he lives; a dying Empire riddled with prejudice and class distinction. The twenty-three scenes cover that career from 1890 until Redl's suicide in 1913—itself a significant date as the eve of the Great War, when Redl's army will actually have to fight and the Empire crumbles. At the beginning of the play the only fighting done by the officers is in duels at dawn. Redl has been asked to appear as a second, along with Steinbauer, for an unpopular officer (a Jew and, as it turns out, a homosexual) who has challenged the aristocratic von Kupfer. While they wait, Redl confesses that he has had a disturbing dream—of being arrested as he visits a friend in jail. Von Kupfer arrives and kills Sicynski. The fact that Redl will have to work very hard lest he end up "in some defeated frontier town with debts" is explored in scene 2 where Lieutenant-Colonel von Möhl warns Redl that appearing as a second for Sicynski did not do his career much good (von Kupfer, as a principal, has certain advantages and can get away with incidents like this occasionally). Von Möhl introduces this in a long description of the army as a place where genuine merit "rarely goes unnoticed or unrewarded." By sheer hard work Redl does begin to rise and this seems to explain why he is unable to enter into the brilliant social life other young officers enjoy. A hovering waiter and Redl's failure to achieve any satisfaction with Hilde are all, however, clues to Redl's real problem. Osborne's problem was that prepublicity made the surprise of discovery impossible and it is difficult to say, once one knows, how surprising the discovery would have been had we entered the theater innocently. Certainly the rise of this promising officer attracts the attention of Colonel Oblensky in the Russian Secret Service, who finds Redl interesting enough to keep him in sight though the only odd detail in his hardworking career is the invention of an uncle who gives him presents. We next see Redl at the Court Ball, a rather stuffy affair in a Vienna where everyone, including the Emperor, is bourgeois. Here he meets the Countess Sophia and the talk ranges over a society and its army still living in the eighteenth century; though, as Hotzendorfer remarks, nothing in the nineteenth century was better and there is no sense that the twentieth century will be an improvement. But they are all living, as Kunz points out, in a charade, pretending to be an Austrian Empire that is little more than a convenience for other nations and which, like the

Hofball, is pretty pointless. For Redl, however, the evening is not pointless since he is sent for by the Archduke Ferdinand, who is the man to watch.

Redl's affair with the Countess is no more successful, sexually, than any of his previous encounters and though the Countess is in love with him, she is also in the pay of Oblensky, who is still trying to discover what it is that really moves Redl. An encounter with a young man in a café ("I know what *you're* looking for") prepares us for the final scene of act 1 where Redl has just had sex with a young private called Paul. Now it is Redl who wants the light on during sex and his cry: "Why did I wait so long" is interrupted by the arrival of four of Paul's friends who beat him up and rob him. As Paul says: "Don't be too upset, love. You'll get used to it." This is not just a good curtain line—but the insight and perception in it are somewhat qualified by the opening scene of act 2, the well-known Drag Ball. Osborne prefaces this with a rather heavy-handed stage direction and a note on the six categories of guests from paid bum boys through discreet drag queens to the ones who arrive in uniform or evening dress. Redl arrives with his latest young friend, Stefan, in uniform (they have just come from the other Ball at the Hofburg), and he is surprised to meet once more Steinbauer and von Kupfer. He seems relaxed and the talk ranges through various thematic topics: the fancy dress nature of the uniform of the Imperial Army, Redl's career (he is now a Colonel in Counter-Intelligence), and the sense that this ball is

> the celebration of the individual against the rest, the us's and the them's, the free and constricted, the gay and the dreary, the lonely and the mob, the little Tsarina there and the Emperor Francis Joseph.[22]

But if barriers are relaxed there are still barriers. Stefan is uneasy (his father is a chef at the Volksgarten restaurant) and thinks the Baron is a snob. This the Baron admits but he also insists that he is a gentleman. There is also the ephemeral nature of such relationships, as beautiful young men grow older. But what is the cure? Redl, we are told, has tried everything including religion, vows, medical advice, and self-exhaustion and other guests offer their experiences of confessing homosexuality to priest and doctor in a respectable society that is flocking to hear the lectures of the extraordinary Dr. Schoepfer, a Jew who sees homosexuals as potential criminals who should be castrated: "a warning symptom of the crisis in, oh, civilization, and the decline in Christian whatnots."[23] Ferdy, weary of all this talk, moves into a series of entrechats and Redl strikes him, then, clicking his heels in the best Establishment manner, leaves. Neither style—Hofburg nor Drag—suits him. A brief glance at these lectures and Dr. Schoepfer's views on homosexuality ("regression to the phallic stage of libido development" which can be traced back to "a flight from incest") leads to the first meeting between Oblensky and Redl. Patiently Oblensky produces evidence of Redl's sexual life—documents, photographs, even, finally, the boater that should hang over his bed, a trophy from the English Ambassador's son and evidence, too, of the debts which the large sum of money handed to Redl will pay off. Treachery, after all, is only part of the game; and to whom should Redl be loyal save himself? Trussler objects that Redl would be unlikely to attend an affair like the Drag Ball, brilliant though it is as a *coup de thèâtre*, and cites this as yet another example of "Osborne's tendency to indulge in instantaneous developments of character, the causes of which he is reluctant to explore."[24] This misses the point. Redl attends both balls in the same fancy dress and is at home at neither, yet he has to continue to live in a society divided between these two views of life (and the Drag Ball is an annual holiday, no more).

Act 3 concentrates on the difficulty of keeping going as a successful officer and homosexual. The debts now are for a succession of young men who will leave for the lure of marriage and "respectability." Stefan has got the Countess pregnant and will marry her but she, Redl insists, will never know the boy as intimately as he does and will merely turn him into another portly, middle-aged father. Mischa has not merely got married but also gone mad. Redl's power has increased, however, and he can send von Kupfer off to St. Petersburg and pay for his successful coup against the Russians by betraying him to the Russians. He also pays for his latest boy, Viktor—though is this, Osborne asks, very different from the marriages discussed in the play where the only way a young officer can get out of debt is by marrying a rich wife? In an angry scene (act 3, scene 5) with Viktor, Redl runs the full gamut of emotions that have never appeared before, except for the brief outburst at the Baron's Ball. When Viktor wants a girl Redl points out that he also wants Redl's style and to be a gentleman. But he is incapable of initiating anything himself:

If the world depended on the Viktors, on people like you, there would be no first moves made, no inexpedient overtures, no serving, no invention, no spontaneity, no stirring whatsoever in you that doesn't come from elsewhere. . . .[25]

But having depicted the gradual degeneration of the beautiful Viktor into an old painted diseased creature with a big bottom, he takes the boy into his arms like a mother; a chilling sight. The accidental discovery of his treachery shakes the Establishment but, like all Establishments both military and political, it will cover the whole matter up. Redl is handed a pistol so that he can do the right thing and, as he shoots himself, the play ends with Oblensky once more reviewing suitable candidates and, rather puzzlingly, turning his attention to Dr. Schoepfer. I say "puzzlingly" because the precise effect of this scene is unclear. Is Osborne commenting on the theory that homosexuals are responsible for their condition and that it leads to unpatriotic acts, or is the Doctor another Jewish climber who can be relied on to betray the Emperor? This ending was altered in the 1983 Chichester production. Oblensky's command: Next ! was changed to: Whose next ? Instead of a photograph of Schoepfer with Stanitsin's description a blank silhouette was thrown up on the screen as the whole cast glided around the stage on the revolve. This change, however, was not reflected in the text as it was re-issued in 1983.

The Problems of *A Patriot for Me*

Here, then, we have an epic play covering twenty-three scenes in the life of Alfred Redl, an officer in the pre-1914 Austro-Hungarian Imperial Army who achieves high rank in spite of being low born, homosexual (and, incidentally, Jewish), who fights his homosexual tendencies, gives in, is blackmailed by the Russians into spying against the Emperor, discovered, and who commits suicide. The modern parallels are obvious (fading Empire, patriotism, talent, blackmail because of sexual preferences). Many critics felt that Redl as presented lacked an introspective side and that Osborne had produced, in Ferrar's words, "a very deliberate, stiff and finally pompous play from the by-ways of history" with a reticent hero "whom Osborne clearly did not know from inside-out."[26]

Again, however, Osborne has structured the play deliberately. In act 1 he presents the impenetrable nature of a man coming to terms with himself and in act 3 the difficulties of living two lives—dual functioning—which drives Mischa into marriage and madness. Many critics were puzzled as to whether it was an attack on homosexuality or a denunciation of a society that sacrificed able men who happened to be homosexual. Martin Esslin felt that if it were the latter the portrayal of society was inadequate. Osborne's knowledge of background was so sketchy that we were left with a Viennese operetta without music.[27]

Of course, the point about the society that Redl lives in is that it is explicitly playing the part of a Viennese operetta—and this shallow, crumbling society does threaten the energy, talent, and invention of a Redl. Like Maitland, with whom he shares a dream about prison in the first scene, he waits for the inevitable.

The biggest fuss about the play was created in the exchange between Mary McCarthy and Kenneth Tynan. McCarthy was given the front page of the *Observer* Supplement (4 July 1965) and asked for a view of the play against the background of Osborne's work to date and she asked the obvious question: why did Osborne write this play and what does he mean to say?

> . . . can it be an anti-militaristic tract which boldly declares that if universal disarmament had been established in 1890 none of these Jews and homosexuals would have had to lead a life of trite glittering pretence? Dr. Schoepfer would have been out of a job, or transferred to geriatrics, and as an additional bonus there would have been no World War I?

In this vein (which journalists would characterize as "good" copy) she proceeded to attack characterization, dialogue, and Redl's dissimilarity with the true Osborne hero, concluding with a fine but fatal flourish that the chief merit of the play was to provide work for homosexual actors or those who could pass for homosexuals.

Tynan responded to this passionately, and it all added to the play's impact on the public without offering much enlightenment on this puzzling play. Osborne, in statements outside his plays, seems not to be very sympathetic to homosexuals (he always calls them "poufs") but then the same could be said about his comments on women and he has married several of them. In his plays he exhibits compassion and understanding of the Michelangelo brigade who may escape the predatory ravages of women but pay a high price for it. Redl is another Osborne hero, a special case. His problem is not a stammer or a father-complex that leads to constipation and the Reformation; it is a strong sexual preference for young men. This preference isolates him in a society which tends to disapprove of the fulfillment of that preference: marriage is a strongly argued case in the play, provided it does not get in the way of a young man's career. Worth is correct in seeing the play as not so much about homosexuality as about a man "who can't find a congenial style to live in. Redl doesn't know where he is at home, all his impulses are at war."[28]

It seems that he might find a way out by recognizing his impulses for what they are, thus at least putting an end to the awful attempts at sexual release with women. But the alternative to the formal Hofburg Ball is the Drag Ball: light, Mozartian, but as alien to Redl's nature as the other. When he tells Viktor, "You want my style," the verb "want" has two meanings: desire and lack. Viktor would like to be like Redl but cannot be. What drives Redl into despair is the lack of response, imaginative and emotional, in all these young men; they satisfy his physical need but beyond that they merely become facsimiles of gentlemen, acquisitive as the society in which they live. This matter of style—a way of speaking and a way of life—finding the role that suits one and one's audience, moves Osborne into the obvious genre: comedy of manners. *A Patriot for Me*, for all its tight-lipped epic form, looks at the basic issues in comedy of manners: the conflict between passions and instincts and the code of behavior by which society regulates or restricts those feelings; the balance between passion and intellect. Before Osborne settled into this form, however, there was a curious diversion in 1966.

A Bond Honoured

A Bond Honoured was produced by the National Theater at Waterloo Road on 6 June 1966. John Elsom suggests that 1966 was a turning point in Osborne's career marked by the death of George Devine, with whom he had formed a close private bond, and the impact of this loss can, perhaps, be seen in *A Bond Honoured*.[29] Osborne's own account of the work for which, as he remarks, he was paid £250—"for a year's work or so this is less than my wife and I were awarded by the National Assistance Board 13 years ago"[30]—is in the note explaining the play. Kenneth Tynan had asked him to adapt a play by Lope de Vega in three acts with an absurd plot, ridiculous characters, and very heavy humor. What interested him was "the Christian framework of the play and the potentially fascinating dialectic with the principal character. So I concentrated on his development (in the original he rapes his sister in the opening moments of the play . . .) and discarded most of the rest, reducing the play to one long act."

In fact the play is published in two acts. Why did Tynan choose this particular play? Lope de Vega was a prolific writer (he is credited with approximately 2,000 plays, of which some 500 survive) and *La Fianza Satisfecha* is not particularly important and, indeed, may not be by him. Osborne says that he worked from a literal translation provided by the theater but Tynan may have been influenced by the publication of Willis Barnstone's translation in *Tulane Drama Review* (7, no. 1 [Fall 1962]). William M. Whitby and Robert R. Anderson, in the introduction to their excellent edition of *La Fianza Satisfecha* (Cambridge University Press, 1971), point out that in this century the play "has been the object of intermittent but increasing attention, culminating in a kind of fervor of interest since the quadricentennial year of 1962," when Barnstone's translation, *The Outrageous Saint*, was published. Barnstone claimed Leonido as an existential hero (so the play adapts in our postwar period with ease "to the concerns and anxieties of our day") and suggests, rather oddly, that if we interpret it on religious grounds it is shocking since this prototype of Don Juan is not sent to Hell. Because of this the work was consigned to oblivion after the seventeenth century. The connection with existentialism seems modish, and to describe the play as shocking is melodramatic. This play appears in the volume about the lives of Saints—Leonido is to become a saint, and the more outrageous his previous life, the more glorious his conversion. A Leonido raging against the world, morality, and religion was obviously an attractive character for Osborne, who has, anyway, always had more than a passing interest in religion—from sainthood in *Epitaph for George Dillon* to *Luther*—and who is still interested in writing a play about Judas in the manner of *Luther*. From his note on the play, however, Osborne's reading of it was careless. Leonido does not rape his sister and his motivation is briskly suggested (and then filled in later), giving Lope a powerful opening—something Osborne could surely appreciate? Barnstone's translation suggests that the play, within its own conventions, could work on the stage. Osborne retains much of the absurd plot but invents four scenes before the opening of the play to "explain" the hero. This leaves him with four scenes in which to cover all the material Lope uses in three acts. These first four scenes show Osborne creating the source of Leonido's feelings. Leonido is a man of energy, kicking his sleeping servant awake and surrounded by sloth. If he lacks sloth he has, he says, the other four Hindu hindrances: craving, ill will, perplexity, and restless brooding. All around him are born old and the system in which he lives seems as indifferent to him as he to it. Virtue, for him, has meant pleasure; he can like no one, not even himself. His motive for anger is that his sister Marcela (who is also, in Osborne, his daughter) has been sleeping with him for years but is now betrothed to Dionisio and, after her marriage, she resists him. Leonido strikes her and Dionisio, insults his father, and leaves. As he sleeps on the beach a Moorish king and his companions attempt to capture him (they are trying to find a Christian for the king's beloved, Lidora) but Leonido mocks the pointlessness of it all by shouting, "Kill the Christian! Kill the Moor!" and overpowers them. Telling the story of his life to the king, he stresses how different he has been from the beginning. When he was born Etna erupted and his mother's breasts were covered in blood; Sicily he sees as "an island of overprotected people" in which the range of possibilities for living shrink every year.[31] So Leonido becomes a Moor, though, like Redl, he discovers that being a Moor means as little as being either Sicilian or Christian. The act ends with a reminder from his servant that he has a debt to pay to Heaven which Leonido says he will settle later.

Act 2 moves to Tunis, where Lidora, a Moorish maid, has fallen in love with Leonido. She asked for a Christian from her lover, the king, but rightly points out he has only brought her another Moor. Leonido, however, will have none of her and threatens, entirely in character, to "bust your law, break your city, strike at friendship and kill your King."[32] Meanwhile, Christian prisoners are brought to the island: Marcela and Leonido's father. Lidora embraces them as her sister and father and begins to learn about the Christian faith. Osborne's heart hardly seems to be in the writing of this résumé of Christian doctrine and he rapidly passes to the moment when Leonido, having beaten his father up and blinded him, goes off to meet the barefoot Shepherd with a bag full of emblematic objects. At the sight of the Cross he falls to the ground and, as the Shepherd leaves, puts on the symbolic garments to become a gentle lamb. In Osborne the epithet is "dismal" and Osborne makes Leonido fight the Moors ferociously before he gives in and confesses his sins. He has raped his mother (but his father raped her, too, to get him) and if Marcela has a child that will be his too. He goads the onlookers on to kill him and the play ends with his epitaph:

Well, King, he played a good tune on vituperation. It may not be a bond honored, but it's a tune of sorts to end with.[33]

Osborne instructed that the play should be acted in a particular way. The actors were to sit in a circle, motionless, rising only when they were to take part in the action, and their acting style was to be "extremely violent, pent-up, toppling on and over the edge of animal howlings and primitive rages" but easy, modern, and natural at the same time.

The Problems of *A Bond Honoured*

The play was performed in a double bill with Peter Shaffer's *Black Comedy*, which helped to ensure audiences, but neither the critics nor the reviewers were particularly impressed. Ferrar finds Osborne uncomfortable with his material and sees the Noh staging as arbitrary and "symptomatic of his awkwardness about what to do with the whole undertaking";[34] Trussler suggests that the adapter tired steadily of a task he had not chosen,[35] while Anderson believes that the play is best forgotten as a misconceived venture from beginning to end.[36] John Russell Taylor remarks that it "need not detain us long" and suggests that the congenial nature of the material results in a kind of parody of Osborne. Critics who knew (or said they knew) the original felt that it would be best to forget it since it was clearly better than the adaptation: Osborne had strained credulity not merely in performance but in the alterations and particularly with the conversion. In Lope de Vega, Leonido meets Christ disguised as a shepherd and is converted, where Osborne's Leonido meets a Christ who seeks retribution without repentance—which, according to Trussler, puts Lope's hero in the New Testament and Osborne's in the Old.[32]

Reviewers were puzzled rather than dismissive,[38] and given the problems of the play the general tone of reviewing was not ungenerous, but the critics received a telegram from Osborne dissolving the gentleman's agreement "to ignore puny theater critics as bourgeois conventions" and declaring "open and frontal war" on them.[39] Charles Marowitz, quoting this telegram, agrees with Osborne that English critics are an odd lot and should be attacked but while he can admire the gesture the play is another matter—"a murky, turgid, over-schematic piece of labored prose that huffs desperately to come to life and hasn't even Osborne's usual bursts of fanged language to recommend it."

Martin Esslin summed up most of the problems cogently in his review in *Plays and Players* (August 1966). He looks at the hero and his story, the suggestions that he is an existential hero, and the source. In Osborne's version a shepherd leaves a sack of emblems of martyrdom which Leonido puts on and then surrenders to the Moors, which makes little sense at all, either logically or existentially. In Lope's version, Leonido tries to bind Christ the shepherd, who disappears to reappear as Christ the Redeemer, carrying His Cross. Before this vision Leonido falls to the ground paralyzed and breaks into a long speech of repentance, contrition, and conversion. Fully a third of the original play depicts the saint. Osborne has added to the play only on the side of wickedness—a long affair with his sister/daughter and the rape of his mother—and cut out repentance so radically that it makes no impact. Lope's religion may not fit Osborne's philosophy and Osborne may interpret the theme any way he wishes, but, in that case, why leave in so much detail and incident from the original, which only makes sense in terms of Leonido's conversion? In Lope's play Leonido finds himself when he realizes the "enormity of his guilt"; in Osborne's version he merely goes "temporarily insane"!

Clearly, such criticism is not pleasant for an author who has worked for over a year on a project (and for a mere £250), but the foray into the world of telegrams and anger did look as if Osborne was insisting on good reviews whatever the quality of his play. An opportunity to judge the original came later that year when, in December, the BBC Third Program broadcast a close translation by Joe Burroughs with the title *A Pledge Redeemed*. Mr. Burroughs stated the message of the play briefly in *Radio Times*: Lope believed in God; he believed that good is greater than evil, that the mercy of God is infinite and that sin is finite.

Reviewing this broadcast in the *Spectator* (6 January 1967) Henry Tube recalled that Osborne had always been the dramatist of his time and place, speaking with the accents "not of anger, which is a key too high for our society, but of irritation . . . so that good, evil, God and sin are conceptions well outside his register." Osborne would have every sympathy with Leonido so long as "he remained impervious to redemption." Tynan may have wanted Osborne to pass beyond the barrier to redemption and extend his range but either he could not or would not do this: Leonido accepts redemption with moans and groans and very bad grace. Where Lope's Leonido strikes at belief, Osborne hits out at conformity; where Lope's hero is contemptuous of goodness, Osborne's hates respectability; where Lope's hero is dedicated to the destruction of honor (in the strong Sicilian sense), Osborne's fights "process" or inertia.

1967, however, also saw Osborne defended by an expert witness. Daniel Rogers, as an Hispanist, can at least claim familiarity with the original, which he thinks is unlikely to be a Lope de Vega play. In his article " 'Not for insolence, but seriously': John Osborne's adaptation of *La Fianza Satisfecha*,"[40] he gathers together all the strands of this tangled incident. Rogers believes that Osborne has used his own or someone else's knowledge of Spanish to come closer to the original than Barnstone's translation, whose existential interpretation, he suggests, would make little sense in the seventeenth century and makes little sense now. The "outrageous" nature of Leonido is less so when seen in the context of other heroes from early seventeenth-century Spanish religious drama and the play is second rate: "The great religious plays are far more subtle, complex and profound." Looking at Osborne's adaptation, he examines the differences (in over six pages of comparison) noting that there are changes but in what direction is unclear, though the change in the play could partly be explained by "reference to the concern which drama since Ibsen has shown for causes rather than consequences of human behavior." Osborne's drama looks back to see how characters have come to be what they are, whereas seventeenth-century Spanish drama was forward-looking, "interested in what characters will do, and what will happen to them next." Rogers believes that Osborne has turned the verse into prose "extraordinarily well" and concludes:

> . . . where Osborne translates he does so with invigorating ruthlessness and a firm grasp of essentials; where he alters the story, he tends to clarify causes but to obscure consequences. He preserves, even intensifies, the religious fervor of the original, but the meaning is radically altered and becomes extremely mysterious. The mystery may be seen by some as a challenge, but Esslin's charge of obscurity must, I think, lie.

Chapter Six
For the Mean Time

Alan Carter claims that *Time Present* and *The Hotel in Amsterdam* carry a joint title, *For the Mean Time*, suggesting both "a temporary stage in Osborne's own development and his sour comment upon the time in which we live."[1] John Lahr feels that at forty-three, Osborne's "literary muscle is turning to flab and ruthless self-examination is going to sleep." For Lahr, *Inadmissible Evidence* is the last flowering before Osborne suffocates. Osborne's anger has outlived its historical moment and the currency of wrath is now spurious. The voices in these plays are not angry, merely dyspeptic and tired—and their creator is out of touch: "the famous writer, posing, hiding, turning that stiff upper lip to conceal—even from himself—rigor mortis."[2] Yet in *Time Present* Pamela faces the death of her father and is as angry with the world around her as ever Jimmy Porter was. She was, it is true, born in India and, through her devotion to her father's acting style, is part of that Imperial Past Jimmy was so ambivalent about, but, like him, she looks back with anger. Of course the preoccupation in both plays with the successful or wealthy, upper-middle-class characters and a return to the old-fashioned play (as in *Epitaph for George Dillon* and *Look Back*)—that bourgeois territory Left-wing dramatists in the 1950s had abandoned forever—came as a shock. It suggested not merely middle age but also that the rebel had become respectable and reactionary. But, as David Hirst points out, *Time Present* offers an attitude common with the two plays that followed it, the belief "that style, manners and breeding are the prerogative of a dying class." But whereas in comedy of manners those who possess style are the winners, in Osborne they are the losers, making Osborne's dramatization of the qualities of refinement more ambiguous "since the sympathy he feels for those people who cultivate them and his parallel contempt for the insensitive boors who invade their lives, is tempered by the fact that it is the latter who are happy and successful."[3]

All three plays concern a group of people who are involved in the death of an older man and who explore their relationships in a fairly static situation. Those critics who complained that Osborne could only write monodramas now found they missed the large central voice, though in the first two plays the action is held together by such a voice.

Time Present

Time Present was first performed at the Royal Court on 23 May 1968, with Osborne's new wife, Jill Bennett, playing the part of Pamela. The action takes place in a flat in Pimlico, belonging to a Socialist MP, Constance, whose marriage has broken up (and whose husband has custody of the child). Pamela is sharing the flat since her last affair, too, broke up. The flat shows the presence of the two women—the tidy politician and the actress camping out in the living room. Critics have observed that there is a faintly lesbian quality to this relationship, but, as far as the play goes, they are just good friends and, indeed, both have sexual relations with Constance's current lover, Murray. The flat at the moment is being used as a kind of waiting room, convenient for the hospital where Pamela's father, Gideon Orme, is dying. As the play opens Edith is taking a cup of tea. She is Pamela's mother but has remarried a Tory politician, by whom she has had two more children, Andrew (doing his duty at the hospital) and Pauline, who arrives almost immediately. Osborne describes Edith as in her late fifties, tired "but alert," and Pauline as "eighteen and pretty." Their desultory conversation fills in some of these relationships and also places Pamela as the kind of actress for whom they do not any longer write parts; she is "a bit special" . . . "not a raving beauty exactly but she's not ugly but you don't quite know what to *do* with her." She is at present umemployed, and, unlike Constance, her career has not been a success.[4] The arrival of Constance pushes on the conversation—mainly about Pamela, who will find life hard after her father dies. Edith admits that she and Pamela are not friends, not, at least, as Edith is friends with her other two children. Pamela "seems in the middle somewhere"—like Archie Rice, she belongs to neither of the groups who know what they are doing. When Pamela enters her first cry is for champagne before she launches into an attack on youth—prompted by the boyfriend, Dave, whom Pauline has tactfully left on the doorstep. But, as Pamela reminds us, she is winding down after attending a performance by Gideon and what she says is part of that process. Pauline, moreover, gives as good as she takes and, since Pauline means what she says, it is Pauline who is bitchy here. Later, after Edith and Pauline have gone, Pamela can remark that Dave is harmless and that when one is young no one really minds if one wears cheap clothes. With Pamela one has to listen to the tone of the voice rather than the content. The context of Pamela's bitchiness appears after Edith and Pauline have gone when Pamela asks why they took so long—talking about going but standing around looking distressed and drinking champagne. Pauline calls Pamela provincial and she agrees. Being born in India and looking back at her father's kind of theater is a disadvantage in the world where she has to live and which she summarizes in her attacks on youth and politicians who make no effort. Neither has style as her Welsh father had. The future terrifies her and she attacks Constance over her pamphlet about "Striding into the Seventies with Labour." Constance points out that it is easy to poke fun at people who are trying to cope with the future but Pamela asks, what about the meantime? She feels stuck in the here and now, where sleep is difficult, where one has to wait up.[5] Here her syntax shows the confusion between waiting for Orme's death and larger issues. In the theater, for example, Abigail is the great success—in a fashionable way—and the fashionable way with plays is now nonverbal: "sort of about leaving nude girls in plastic bags at railway stations."[6] Constance's politics is showbusiness, too, and requires her to believe in, or pretend to believe in, phrases like public spending, private sector, incentive and exports, "productivity, exploiting our resources to the full, readjustment."[7] This last word carries the key to the problem. Readjustment. What, in such a world, Pamela asks, will happen to Constance's child? Statistics suggest, to Constance, that he is more than likely to go to University but for Pamela, having "A" levels means that they will want to make a University Challenger out of him!

Murray, Constance's lover, arrives. Abigail phones from her dress rehearsal and finally Edward turns up. Pamela despairs of going to bed (she has, after all, to sleep in the living room) but as Murray and Constance go to bed she settles down with Edward. The two seem of an age—that age is the early thirties—and at ease with one another. They browse through Gideon's cuttings book. Katharine Worth, who feels that Pamela must be a rather remote figure for most people, suggests that it is hard to envisage Gideon's style from the titles—"*The Real Thing*"—or to enter sympathetically into her nostalgia for it.[8] But that style recalls, surely, someone like Donald Wolfit, the last of the great actor-managers who took theater to the people before it was centralized and subsidized in London. And if the treatment of bears and squirrels was ambivalent at the end of *Look Back* the irony here, too, is unmistakable. Pamela and Edward are having fun (Pauline accused Pamela of hating any sort of fun) recalling, with affection, these ridiculous plays, and when Pamela is momentarily off her guard, the telephone rings to tell her that Gideon is dead. Bad timing, she says, the response of an actress to the whole situation of being born.

Simon Trussler has attacked the clumsiness of the exposition in this act (though he also, curiously, describes Pauline as "pallid"); the first twenty minutes, he says, are very nearly disastrous as Edith and Pauline fill in background with which both are already acquainted. Since Edith is not a gossip, this conversation is extraneous. Similarly the characterization of Constance is inadequate and Osborne shows a remarkable lack of interest in the political side of the play, even referring to a bill as an act.[9] This last detail is as worrying as striking clocks in *Julius Caesar* but the comments on the clumsiness of the exposition are a response to the awkwardness of the early part of the act. They do, however, overlook the context. This group of people is in the artificial situation of waiting for death. They assemble from a mixture of motives. Edith, for example, is answering the call of duty while Pauline, who has no duty to be there, seems to do it from affection for her mother. They pass the time talking about things they already know because, frankly, that is what often happens to people in such a situation. The so-called clumsiness portrays Osborne's recognition that the hospital situation is a tense, awkward experience that brings out the best and the worst in people. The characters on the stage are much less alive than Gideon Orme and this is entirely right, an effect Osborne works for rather than blunders into. Pamela is asking for style and he surrounds her with various examples of people living without it, successful, even happy, in a world where Pamela feels lost.

In act 2, some weeks later, she is still lost and, as it turns out, pregnant as well. Again we have the typical Osborne situation in which a group of people is genuinely concerned for the heroine and is rejected by her. Edith and Pauline, returning from the Orme Memorial Service, are distressed to find her in her nightdress in the late afternoon, keeping going on sleeping pills with the telephone switched off. She has been like this since the funeral and Edith is naturally worried. Pamela is unemployed and has few friends. Even her homosexual friends have given her up except for her agent Bernard. Constance will probably marry Murray and Pamela must think about what is to happen to her. She has neither husband, children, nor career and though, for the first time, she has been stirred into sexual life, her response is to arrange an abortion. She will not live with Murray or bear his child though she will help him with his play and his relationship with Constance; but what she does has nothing to do with either of them. As Worth reminds us, this is not quite the conventional, child-free world of Coward. In Osborne characters have to suffer consequences just like ordinary people; indeed Osborne's point is that they suffer them more in every way:

> Pamela suffers in her imagination with her father who is dying in a hospital while she fights her rearguard action on behalf of his style. . . .[10]

Pamela will certainly not hurt Constance by telling her the truth or by staying with Murray; she will not even hurt Constance when that lady arrives, typically, with the wrong kind of champagne.

Abigail's play has, of course, been a success. This gives Osborne a chance to poke fun at the critics' responses—it is a Rattigan-type play—"finely wrought and blessedly well constructed," which, as Pamela says, means that "it's like a travelling clock. You can see all the works. That way you know it must keep the right time."[11] As Pamela prepares to leave, Abigail and Edward arrive, having spent the day celebrating Abigail's success—shopping, going to a Swedish movie, and dressing up. Abigail should have read a lesson at Orme's memorial service. And it was Edward's idea that they should drop in to see if Pamela is all right. He cares. Abigail's performance is larger than life but it is, as Pamela concedes, alive. After they have gone Constance is prepared for a long emotional encounter but, again, Pamela takes refuge in the cuttings book, *"The Real Thing,"* until Bernard arrives to collect her. The play ends as Constance telephones Murray to come to dinner, echoing the words used by Pamela when she tried to write letters to a lover in act 1.

Critical Reaction to *Time Present*

The disadvantage of having, for the first time, a central character who was a woman was, according to Esslin in *Plays and Players* (July 1968), that "what passes for anger with Jimmy Porter looks awfully like bitchiness with Pamela. Even when it isn't." This is to listen only on the most superficial level to what she is saying and feeling but perhaps it explains why many critics did not feel that Pamela mattered. A more positive approach is taken by Ferrar, who suggests that Osborne is beginning to ask the question, how are we to avoid ending up as a Maitland or a Pamela? "In her final calm acceptance of nothingness Osborne is showing the erosion of human richness through a kind of insane non-attachment."[12] Such a response is preferable to those who dismissed the play because nothing happens: "Nothing happens in all these plays. Each is essentially a monologue in which Osborne has casually mismanaged structure and the suspension of disbelief. Everything is tired, verbose, and bathetic."[13] Such a judgment from Lahr comes as no surprise but John Russell Taylor falls into the same cliché, saying that nothing happens in *Time Present*. Nothing happens in *Waiting for Godot,* twice, but we think no less well of the play. Taylor does, however, see a new departure here. Though both plays have a central character, the basis of the drama is a pattern of social and emotional relationships, but he does not feel Osborne handles them successfully and the price we pay for them is that the diatribes, too, seem "half-hearted and perfunctory," as if they were there to meet audience expectation rather than coming out of the author's feeling. He finds Pamela too typical, another essentially unlikable character presented as if she were sympathetic. Like Leonido, though on a smaller scale, she constantly asks to be judged.[14]

This seems to miss the energy and the pain and the fun of her character. The language should provide a clue. Kennedy, writing about Pamela's language, suggests that she projects herself in terms of two opposed theatrical styles:

> . . . the twittering world of "Show-business," which now embraces "everybody," and the moribund theater and life-style of her dying father. What verbal vitality there is in this ill-organized play comes from the way Pamela sees the world as a stage and dramatizes her negatives, as she parodies the vocabulary and gestures of a "mean Time."[15]

Kennedy compares her to Beckett's Winnie: Pamela sets the old style which he defines as "a collection of stale captions, with bits of cliché dialogue from hack plays. . . ." This, of course, misses the tone and hardly allows style to be anything more than the words on the page.

Pamela's responses are sharp, brisk and often witty and she admits that wit "very often is petty." Many of her epigrams (she really is allowed a long speech very seldom)—"excessive effort is vulgar"—are challenged and qualified. When Murray accuses her of treating other people as if they were not there, as if they were walk-ons, we are reminded of *Inadmissible Evidence*. Pamela's breakdown is not so obvious because she alone recognizes the death of Orme as something more than a funeral and a memorial service. She seeks the grace of detachment; but as she speaks of this she and her world are breaking down. Where Jimmy measured people by their emotional commitment, Pamela judges them by restraint. She walks out, saving Constance at least (as Maitland begs his wife not to be involved with him at the end of *Inadmissible Evidence*), but otherwise she cannot, will not, adjust. The price of style, then, is too high and we should grieve that Pamela has to pay it.

The Hotel in Amsterdam

Alan Carter has dubbed this play "Six Characters searching for an identity lost on the road to success"[16] but then spoils the effect by suggesting that Osborne is more concerned here with friendship and goodness than in any of his previous plays. What he should say is that these things tentatively exist here whereas the quest for them has haunted all the previous plays. Certainly here we have, unequivocally, a group of characters who talk to one another—even Laurie talks with his friends, not at them—and language is a means of communication rather than a weapon or a strategy. Trussler sees the end of the play as a choice—freedom or disintegration now their common bond of hatred has gone[17]—but this overlooks the bonds of guilt. Though this group of friends is bound by love, affection, or habit, they are also held together, particularly at the end of the play, by a shared sense of betrayal. The play, moreover, looks at the group on holiday, trying to insulate themselves from lives to which they must return at the end of the play. Unlike Pamela, life goes on for them; unlike Pamela, these friends may be lost on the road to success but they are lost together and the road leads them toward success, whereas Pamela is alone on the road to failure. So the play is a step forward for Osborne, even as it recalls the "success" of Luther, who ends up comfortable and triumphant but still gnawed by doubt and fear.

The Hotel in Amsterdam opened on 3 July 1968 at the Royal Court, directed by Anthony Page, with Paul Scofield in the role of Laurie. It looks at the beginning and end of a long weekend spent by a group of friends escaping from a monster employer, the kind of monster, one suspects, who has usually occupied the center of the stage in previous Osborne plays. Three couples, Laurie and Margaret (who is pregnant), Gus and Annie, and Dan and Amy, have just arrived at their suite in a large, first-class hotel in Amsterdam and the whole of act 1 is devoted to establishing the relationships in this group and watching them settle in. The brief introduction of a porter or a waiter allows Osborne to explore the various ways in which each can or will not cope with organizing the holiday (it soon becomes clear that if Laurie can get away with not doing something he will), a holiday they regard as a great escape from their employer, K. L.—"the biggest, most poisonous, voracious, Machiavellian dinosaur in the movies."[18] The escape is not without guilt, is founded on deceit, and leads to various attempts at self-justification—they are all conspirators, with Amy, K. L.'s secretary, as "the real Judas." Osborne follows up this reference with an extended analogy with the Crucifixion (cocks crowing and denying Christ) and at the end of the act curses K. L. for having used them in his worthless world. Typically this curse predicts the actual end suffered by K. L. but, two lines later, Laurie says that he is probably the only one who believed all that. It was a performance among friends—"near or around forty but none middle-aged" who are pretty flashy and vigorous looking—and though Laurie's arias are reminiscent of the tirade they take place with an audience that cooperates. The group passes the time amiably discussing the class system, working-class mothers, pursuing in-jokes about El Fag airlines or the kind of animal each of them resembles if K. L. is a dinosaur. The group is also aware that it is slowing down. Details like the poor quality of sleep, losing vitality, even losing names from an address book after every Christmas are part of their life now. Laurie is, however, serious about the business of writing. He sees himself as a conjuror without white tie and tails, putting his hand out into the air and producing—air. Which Margaret swiftly deflates with the comment: Hot.[19] Yet there is surely a touch of autobiographical bite when Laurie complains about working so hard and being written off "as not fulfilling my early promise by some philistine squirt drumming up copy."[20] He also appreciates the rareness of the occasion:

How often do you get six people as different as we all are still all together, all friends, and who all love each other? After all the things that have happened to us. Like success to some extent, making money—some of us. It's not bad.[21]

Such a mood can survive the differences among them if each is careful not to go too far—hence the restraint of the love declared between Annie and Laurie which closes the act as the snow begins to fall. Plot, clearly, is minimal, though with *Look Back* in mind we can foresee that Laurie's curse will be fulfilled and references to Margaret's sister, Gillian, prepare us for her arrival in act 2.

Act 2 is two evenings later and opens on a relaxed note. The holiday has been a success, so much so that Laurie wants them to stay on an extra day or go back and live together in some broken-down Victorian castle to continue their freedom from K.L., nagging relations, a world that requires you to adjust to it but is never prepared to adjust to you. Laurie's parody of a letter from those relations is beautifully written, capturing the tone exactly—depressing and funny. It is a world, however, from which one can only have the briefest of holidays. The arrival of Gillian, who pretends to be bright, brave, and interested, shatters the mood. Laurie, at last, begs her to break into tears. Jokes from Laurie no longer keep the holiday mood going. The open declaration of the love between Annie and Laurie is made in the knowledge that nothing can be done about it without hurting other people. Gillian cannot bear to be alone and neither, it appears, can K.L. The telephone rings to announce that he has killed himself, with their telephone number, which he got from Gillian, on the blotter on his desk. Laurie has said that he will never come back to this hotel or Amsterdam because it was the place where he spoke of his love for Annie; as the friends prepare to leave, the question of their return recurs. It is unlikely that they will come here again: "But I expect we might go somewhere else"—or so Laurie hopes.

Criticism of *The Hotel in Amsterdam*

Harold Hobson was enthusiastic in the *Sunday Times* (7 July 1968):

. . . the best contemporary play in London: the richest in wit, the most arresting in mood, the most accomplished in performance, and (what is still more important) the most far-reaching and haunting in resonance . . . It is about fear, sometimes well founded but more often not, that seizes on people in middle life, when the future no longer seems bright and certain before them. It is about friendship. It is about goodness.

Benedict Nightingale, in *Plays and Players* (September 1968), was less enthusiastic. At least half of his review was about the creative process, Mr. Osborne, and the critics—matters that are, admittedly, in the play. When he passes to the play itself he sees it as better than *Time Present:*

> It is a sort of tone-poem, reflecting mood and atmosphere—the mood of a group of six friends abroad, all self-conscious and a bit jaded, film people unsuccessfully trying to forget the pressures from which they are escaping; sitting about, chatting about nothing in particular, drinking whiskey, wondering what to do next. . . .

But the friends are not unsuccessful in escaping; the process takes place between the acts (they are, after all, only unpacking in act 1) and just as they have succeeded Gillian arrives and shatters the created harmony, which can hardly be described as "a rather negative thing, based on a collective escape from common pressures."

From this point Nightingale moves into familiar territory: Laurie is too large a character for his function in the play but at least he is a character; the others hardly come to life and exist only in relation to Laurie, who anyway sounds too much like Osborne. Possibly Scofield's magnetic personality did attract too much attention. When Helen Dawson visited the play (*Plays and Players,* February 1969) the role had been taken over by Kenneth Haigh (the original Jimmy Porter), who tackled it in a different way. Now the jokes "seem to be drawn out of despair," a Jimmy Porter who has grown up and made it in the film world, no longer angry but "still fighting the taste of emptiness which even 'success' has left":

> Haigh's Laurie is always waiting for something . . . this is why he is surrounded by his friends, for how else would he be able to hang on, perhaps for the rest of his life? In this way the other characters in the play become more than mere props, an audience or line-feeders.

Michael Anderson found it an attractive but rather slight play; Osborne allowing himself the indulgence of playing. The conversation is "insubstantial but enjoyable"—and this possibly encouraged him not to listen to it very carefully since he decides that the melodramatic ending is unfortunate: K.L.'s death and the idle conversation that precedes it "do little to illuminate one another."[22] Little of this idle conversation rang true to the ears of John Russell Taylor though he concedes that in Laurie Osborne has created a character who moves beyond the "merely vituperative range of the 'typical' Osborne hero to admit involvement in others and even compassion for them, as well as for himself" which may, or may not, suggest a new maturity in Osborne.[23] Both seem to have missed the point which may not be entirely a critical fault but some response to the social context of the characters. Osborne's aristocrats are now socially aristocratic, too, though they pay a price for exclusiveness which is darker than one expects in a Coward-like comedy. The group, as Worth notes, has come to relax out of K.L.'s reach:

> They can't quite shake him off, though: the strain of trying and not succeeding is very much in the play, as well as the rather touching sense of ease and warmth which—in the first London production . . . spread across the stage as the weekend took its course. Laurie, the writer/entertainer at the center of the play, is the magician who works the charm. . . .[24]

Laurie may sound like Pamela but, unlike her, he has an audience who "understand the content of tone of voice." They also understand and sympathize with the pain of the struggle to be jokey even when the romantic feeling creeps in and is declared; they move toward tentative communion which, as Laurie says, is rare, bloody unnatural. This counts for nothing for those who see the Angry Young Man changed into Colonel Blimp. Thus Lahr comments: "The people who clutter this play are rich, successful, bored, and too tired to fight."[25]

Frank Marcus saw the play as Osborne standing still while he caught his breath: "He upholds the virtues of friendship, honesty, propriety, and self-knowledge. They are middle-aged virtues, but that does not invalidate them."[26] Only the cult of youth, which has always worried Osborne from *Epitaph for George Dillon* onward, would and does despise middle-aged virtues. We thrilled to Jimmy's cry for life and enthusiasm but then we have to ask about the quality of life and the ends to which enthusiasm is put. Laurie, like Pamela, uses repartee to cover up insecurity and unhappiness and the terror that his magic—producing something out of the air—will fail. He is, however, unlike Pamela, a member of a group which understands, shares his fear, and talks to him. The longer speeches stand out as "turns" from an entertainer, to keep them going. D. L. Hirst argues that the threats to this delicate achievement—from the waiter to the omnipresent K.L.—finally take shape with the arrival of Gillian, whose unhappiness is neither funny nor stylish. Laurie's attack is on her crude, selfish emotionalism, her bad manners. Laurie's ability to shape feeling through language is nowhere better exhibited than in his declaration of love, but when Annie reciprocates, breeding and language merge into a discussion of the weather in London. The fellowship is too important for any member of the group to destroy it through selfish or thoughtless conduct.[27] This sense of the group persists in the next play; it does not, however, return to Amsterdam; it spends Christmas west of Suez.

West of Suez

West of Suez opened at the Royal Court on 17 August 1971. It was directed by Anthony Page and the cast included Ralph Richardson and Jill Bennett. The title recalls Kipling's "Mandalay" and the balmy days of Empire in a time when Britain no longer maintains a presence east of Suez. Osborne intended to write it at first in the epic style, with the lowering of the Union Jack and a native band, but he felt that this would be overindulging himself in the tricks of the epic theater which had worked so well in *The Entertainer*.[28] In fact he gets this scene in as recollected by one of the residents, Lamb. The play is set "on a sub-tropical island, neither Africa nor Europe, but some of both, also less than both," and when Osborne was asked where the play was set he replied briefly:

> In the middle of the Twentieth Century. It is an amalgam of many such places I've been to, including the French South Pacific.[29]

Instead of a flag-lowering ceremony Osborne opens the play with a long conversation between two of the visitors, Frederica and Edward. After this conversation Edward disappears from the play and only reappears to pronounce the final line; the epitaph for Wyatt Gillman. This in itself should alert us to the fact that this opening conversation is more than just exposition, though, as usual, Osborne has burdened himself with a great deal of that. The scene is vague but the time is precise; it is just after Christmas in the middle of the twentieth century. The Brigadier is taking his mother to the airport (she is apparently frightful, as mothers tend to be at this stage of Osborne's work) and Wyatt has been spending the holiday there with his daughter Robin, who lives with the Brigadier (Patrick is still married, with two children, but divorce is impossible). The other three daughters have also gathered for the holiday: Evangie, the intellectual; Mary, who is married to Robert, a teacher in the North Country; and Frederica, who is married to Edward, a pathologist. Wyatt has also brought his secretary, Christopher. Various other characters drop in for lunch or dinner: the girls' homosexual hairdresser, Alastair, who brings a young American, Jed; Owen Lamb, a successful writer living in tax exile on the island; and Harry, an American, who also lives on the island. No one seems to be enjoying the holiday particularly (except Robert) and the group has little to do except sit and talk and drink or swim. The long opening conversation between Edward and Frederica establishes where we are, with whom, and why. It also establishes the mood and begins to prepare us for the symbolic implications of this group. From the individual, Pamela, Osborne moved to a group of friends and he now uses that group, this time a family, to represent aspects of Western culture and civilization. Thus Edward moves out of the action because he is not part of the family's imperial memory. And yet he should be. Wyatt was born in Srinigar, Kashmir (*his* father was in the Colonial Service), and his daughters Robin and Frederica were born in Kandy (Ceylon) while Evangie was born in Singapore. The Brigadier was born in Mesopotamia and even Owen Lamb is part of the group since he was born in Kuala Lumpur. Robert, Mary's husband, had to make do with Hastings but he copes. As an outsider he is fascinated by the four sisters—"an inner circle of lives"—so much so that he says he is almost tempted to try each one in turn. Edward was born in Rangoon but he remembers the colonial days as having taken away his sense of humor. When Frederica says they are not forgotten he replies that what they are remembered by now is the buildings, as history for tourists who leave their litter, and by "package smiles and surliness and black feeling all round. . . ."[30] Edward, not just as a pathologist, is a "blood and shit" man and it is entirely appropriate that he spends much of the play on the beach with Jed.

Osborne's problem was to combine a well-made play about personal life with an epic play which had wider proportions. He needed the epic texture because the play is about, as he sees it, the decline of Western civilization, but he needed the concentration of the well-made play to examine the privilege of idleness, if it is, indeed, a privilege. The opening talk between Frederica and her husband establishes that this is an island where sores do not heal; and conversation about sleep and birds allows the speakers to think back to England and of England from an island that is a mixture of lethargy and hysteria, brutality and sentimentality, craven, but pleased with itself. Edward tries to use language as inventively as Frederica (her relish for words appears in the opening remark about a slow waiter—"They're not waiters for nothing") but basically he stays a blood and shit man. Of one of his long sentences he admits that he cannot understand it but "there was some bacteria jumping about in there if you can be bothered and we neither of us can."[31] As the group assembles the couple are joined by Mary and Robert, then Robin and her Brigadier, and they discuss writing (both Wyatt and Evangie are writers); we even have a quotation from Jimmy Porter! Christopher and Evangie drift in and, finally, Wyatt Gillman himself, one of those lovable monsters Osborne likes to create and which, one suspects, are loosely based on himself: "All my life people have been telling me I'm quite nice really, as if they expected me to kick them in the crotch."[32] Wyatt Gillman projects exactly the same note of surprise and self-satisfaction. His parents were in the Colonial Service but he chose literature rather than service. He did not even serve in the war (the first of four wars as Osborne reminds us).

Other guests arrive. Alastair brings a young American called Jed (a student—to which Wyatt responds by asking him if he is eternal) and there comes also a successful writer, Lamb. The party is completed by the arrival of Harry, who complains that he is tired and blames it on living on the island. Wyatt laments the cold and damp of England, which he misses but wishes he did not, and closes his eyes against the sun.

Act 2 opens as Wyatt and a few of the guests relax after lunch; a drowsy time when the talk is of memories. For Robert—and we see why he is enjoying his Christmas—memory means school playgrounds, frozen lavatories, and Irish stew, but for Lamb and Wyatt the memories of England are more congenial—tea at the Ritz, Covent Garden, Blackfriars Station, even George Moore's underpants. Boredom can only be tempered with talk but when Wyatt comes up with a jingle and is applauded he rejects the jingle and the applause. He was using words as chatter, which is a sin against words; and a sin against words is a sin against God. He then protests that he is pompous, but this self-conscious deflation does not remove the seriousness.

Language is to be used to shape feeling, to exhibit shared feeling and pain as we see in the memory games the family now play, games that lead to Lamb's recollection of the hand-over of power. When the pain and despair in this memory become too great for Lamb it is Wyatt who tries to modulate a pain that is too deep for words into a comedy of situation. But Lamb goes on about the unhappiness of those left behind—himself, Alastair, even Jed—the lack of shared experience which strengthens as well as becomes exclusive, and Wyatt again distracts with quotations from a newspaper. Lamb recovers and, talking with Frederica, says how much he admires her performance and at the same time her honesty (it is Frederica who remarks that Harry is not tired but is dying).

The arrival of an interviewer, Mrs. James, from the local newspaper gives Wyatt a chance to perform, too. Mrs. James has been created, perhaps, a shade too sharp but this only makes Wyatt work even harder at his performance. She refuses to play the game and so Wyatt, like Jimmy Porter, grows more outrageous. The interview also gives Osborne an opportunity to comment on his usual themes—the critics, mankind, the English imagination and genius. Wyatt makes it clear that he is playing a game—his epigrams on man and Utopia show this. And his view of the island recalls words used by Edward and Frederica at the beginning of the play, as does his definition of himself as "just a lot of hot shit . . . blood, vanity and a certain prowess." The real sin in life he sees as "the incapacity for proper despair."[33] His mood darkens as he expresses a fear not of death but of ludicrous death, which he feels is in the air. Two tourists stray into the garden at this moment and break the mood; they also liberate some anger in Frederica which is turned on her father, who can do what he likes and expects everyone to be amused by the humor of it, the eccentricity. Wyatt, however, claims the privilege of a clown.

The second scene opens to music—no longer the Beethoven of *Heartbreak House* but a "strange noise of resentful-sounding music." In a quiet moment Christopher and Frederica talk. Christopher, who has left his wife, child, and house and now looks after Wyatt, recognizes the pain that she feels. Jed enters, reminding Christopher of a young SS officer he had killed in his war. Earlier in the play Robert had remarked that if you could get Jed to speak he would be someone who would sin against language, the language of the King James Bible and Cranmer's prayer book. Jed, who has not said two words so far in the play, now speaks. He attacks them, moving rapidly from

"I" to "we." The attack is memorable and painful—as if Jimmy Porter had been compelled to use only monosyllables in his tirades. Yet the impression that he uses only four-letter words is just that, an impression. The speech is angry and it makes its point: they are all useless, they and their culture and their precious words which, like them, will now be abolished:

> There's only one word left and you know what it is. It's fuck, man. Fuck. . . . That's the last of the English for you babies. Or maybe shit. Because that's what we're going to do on you. Shit. . . . And there's nothing, not nothing you or anybody else can do about it. . . . So all you'd better do, all you *will* do, is die, die, baby. And pretty soon.[34]

Wyatt, once more refusing to hear what he does not want to hear, rises to go to bed as islanders enter "out of the darkness" pointing guns at the group. As Wyatt turns to run they shoot him, leaving Edward to pronounce his epitaph: "My God—they've shot the fox. . . ."

The strongest sense from this play is neither boredom nor anger; it is betrayal. The Judas image had appeared in *The Hotel in Amsterdam,* and when the time is right Osborne will write his play about Judas, about "a feeling of betrayal that is uppermost among middle-aged people today. There is a terrible resentment towards young people and, of course, blacks. But I don't think people who are truly adult ever feel threatened in that way."[35]

Critical Response to *West of Suez*

As Michael Anderson points out once more we have a group on holiday, this time on an unnamed island that was, until recently, a British colony; once again a writer dominates the play and there is an unexpected death at the end, but here, much more than in *The Hotel in Amsterdam,* the main preoccupation is England. Curiously Anderson finds the group relaxed, with nothing to do but drink and talk, and also finds Wyatt Gillman one of Osborne's most likable protagonists, but neither observation is entirely supported by the text. What is undeniable, however, is that Wyatt is both a personality and representative, a patriot but one whose patriotism is "almost exclusively concerned with feelings, memories, subtle gradations of the emotions," which leads inevitably to the theme of language—the language Jed destroys. Osborne has little liking for this character, who, according to Anderson, is allowed to shock but denied psychological sympathy. The line about the fox Anderson interprets as an example of Osborne's liking for a good ending, one apparently full of significance but tenuous in its connection with the play. Doubtless Osborne intended Wyatt to represent a civilization that can spur its opponents into opposition—Jed in one way, the islanders in another—rejecting civilization and choosing barbarism and chaos: "But Osborne is not a thesis dramatist, carefully preparing each step of an argument to be clinched by the curtain line, and it would be unwise to probe too deeply into the 'meaning' of this final line."[36] It works in the theater, we could say, and that is all that matters. But it is also true that as the final note of a puzzling play it has resonances that can be disturbing. Fox hunting as part of civilization, for example, might disturb some people. It is this final line, then, which clinches the argument for John Lahr, who sees the play as being not about tragedy but merely bad form in a play shaped by Osborne's current obsessions: fame, nostalgia, and boredom.[37]

Manners, of course, as in Jane Austen and Fielding, are outward signs, and the collapse of language must be disturbing. Jed can find no words for his anger in contrast with the command displayed by Wyatt or the relish of Jimmy Porter and his attack in matter and method is a total denial of the values represented by Wyatt "and the physical violence manifested in the senseless murder of the artist is its inevitable and instantaneous corollary."[38] Many critics have, however, complained about the arbitrary association of the Gillman family, in spite of their cruelty and impotence, with humane values before the world is taken over by young Americans and militant blacks. This association is not, surely, the triumph of sentimentality and nostalgia which is said to run through Osborne's work; rather it is his customary recognition that we have inherited pain and impotence. The painful nature of that inheritance is indicated by the form the play takes—its obvious echoes of *Heartbreak House* without a voice to exhort: Learn navigation or be damned. Such a voice would now come too late. In both plays leisurely discussion is brought to an end by sudden violence and death. Surprisingly, Katharine Worth finds Shaw's violence more compelling,[39] though it is decidedly mitigated (and socially very discriminating), and it is Shaw's voluptuaries, spared by the optimist in 1916, who live on to commit the mistakes which will leave Osborne's group in the position they now find themselves. And in Osborne the violence is, surely, not unexpected—it seems more than possible from the opening scene.

The critics who disliked the play did so for what it was saying rather than for the way it was said. Benedict Nightingale suggested in the *New Statesman* (27 August 1971) that it really was as if Jimmy Porter had accepted a knighthood and become jointmaster of the Quorn while Mary Holland, in *Plays and Players* (October 1971), regretted that this High Tory Osborne could not share the wide humanity with which his model Chekhov was endowed, to present the fears of those to be dispossessed and the aspirations of those who will take over:

> More important, he gives no dignity, nothing for mourning to the world which is passing and which *must* pass to open the way for what is to come. When violence erupts on the stage it is casual, irrelevant, without meaning.

It is interesting that Holland believes that violence can be meaningful (and "irrupts" would be preferable to "erupts") but her comparison with Chekhov is as useful as that with Shaw. Osborne is obviously in counterpoint to these dramatists; unlike them he cannot let his characters escape or have much dignity (that is the cruel truth that defies nostalgia): it is the characters in Chekhov and Shaw who have trapped his characters. And where the future is Jed and the end of language and the feelings it can contain, the widespread sympathy for which Chekhov and Shaw are praised would be pointless.

Most critics, however, saw the play as a distinct advance. J. W. Lambert, in the *Sunday Times* (22 August 1971), called it "a great bound forward" while Helen Dawson, in the *Observer* (22 August 1971), described it as "a brave and loving play." For Sheridan Morley, *West of Suez* was "a potent, thoughtful and eminently entertaining evening in the theater" though it was not an easy play. Here, at last, was the old man offstage in *Time Present;* Wyatt Gillman is a traveler in time:

> he sees the present in the awful, dry insecurity of his children, their loveless marriages and hopeless self-destroying quests for a direction in which to steer their drifting lives; and in a final melodramatic flash he sees a future which can find no place for him.[40]

He rightly detects the ghosts of Shaw, Chekhov, and Coward at this banquet—all verbal dramatists; but after the words only the sound of gunfire remains. These people, as John Edmunds points out, have reached a point where they can do nothing but talk and suffer.[41]

Chapter Seven
A Sense of Detachment

West of Suez led Michael Billington to predict that Osborne now stood on the "threshold of greatness" and was about "to enter on his richest period as a dramatist."[1] Certainly his next play showed all the signs of his concern for dying excellence, in and out of the theater, and could be taken either as "a reaching-out, a development of talent . . . a seminal point in Osborne's career"[2] or as proof of the complete disintegration of his talent.[3] Either way it was not a commercial success, though this may be as much a reflection on audiences as on Osborne. In 1961 he had pleaded for the artist's right to play[4] and *A Sense of Detachment,* without plot or characters, is Osborne at play, and frequent references in his autobiography (which covers the years 1929–1956 only) suggest that it is a play for which he has some affection.[5] It may, as some critics suggest, owe something to Handke's *Publikumsbeschimpfung* but it is also unmistakably Osborne. Of course, insulting an audience is a hazardous business, so when the play opened on 4 December 1972 anything could have happened.

A Sense of Detachment

The curtain rises on a stage empty except for a projection screen, a barrel organ, and a piano; the six actors walk on carrying their chairs. They are not characters though the CHAP and his FATHER and GRANDFATHER do introduce the idea of family (the FATHER however died in 1940) and the OLDER LADY and the GIRL offer a woman's point of view; the CHAIRMAN is vaguely in charge. Various remarks such as "Is it all going to be as formless as this?" remind us that the actors are acutely aware of the improvisatory nature of what they are doing, while lines like "You try learning the bloody stuff" point up the essentially phony nature of so-called improvisation. However, the company "improvise" on a number of topics—Scots, Americans, Europe, theatrical devices, theater programs, critics, TV chat shows and audiences—assisted by projections on the screen and suitable music until they conclude act 1 by singing a version of "Widdicombe Fair" in which Harold Pinter is asked to lend his gray mare to carry an assortment of dramatists to Printing House Square. The device that gives momentum to the act is the use of two interrupters. One, an average theatergoer, perhaps, who complains about the bad language and, rightly, supposes that there will be no plot and that Joan Littlewood had done it all years ago, moves, at will, between the stalls and the circle. The other interrupter is in the Stage Box, a drunken football fan who should really be at Drury Lane but has paid his money and is determined to get its worth. He participates to the full and is a glorious creation. These planted interrupters are supposed to encourage the audience to join in, and Osborne instructs the actors that they must be ready for this. He even prepares a list of possible retorts for them—a compendium of comments Osborne must have heard over and over again at his plays.[6]

When the audience return for act 2—if indeed they do return, as Osborne remarks—they find the auditorium flooded with very loud pop music. The interrupters settle down—the Stage Box Man with his crate of brown ale—and the actors return. The device of interruption has now lost its force and interruption now seems like part of the script (as it is). The CHAP passes time by telling us about his life, which, with dreary wives and particularly actresses, seems at times suspiciously close to that of the author while the rest of the actors move into a parody of a TV Chat Show (FATHER, who died before television, asks what on earth they are doing). The Interrupter, too, wants to know who they are and what they are doing! As the sex life of the CHAP falters the OLDER LADY begins to read from a catalog of pornographic books—assisted by screen projections and "appropriate" music. The screen projections are, of course, innocent. As OLDER LADY "gently" declaims "Anal Fuck" we see a fairly pretty contemporary girl, and an episode with skin divers is illustrated by skin divers! The music is variously Handel, *Der Rosenkavalier, Cosí Fan Tutte,* Elgar, or hymns. Modern sex is contrasted with Elizabethan love lyrics and other poetry until a pulpit is wheeled in and CHAP and GIRL move on to the Irish question, the place of women in society, and the absence of love in our modern society, which is dominated by economic unions. These do not love, they amalgamate:

> We are not language. We are lingua. We do not love, eat or cherish. We *exchange*. Oh yes: we talk. We have words, rather: environment; pollution; problems; *issues*. . . .[7]

As CHAP and GIRL proclaim their love the Chairman draws the proceedings to a close with the singing of "Widdicombe Fair" in its original version and dismisses the audience with an ironic blessing.

The critics were not impressed. Thus Irving Wardle, in *The Times* (5 December 1972), felt that this piece could be regarded as "a terminal point of Osborne's derision which has spread from the world outside to the theatrical process itself" while Ronald Bryden, in *Plays and Players* (February 1973), found it even more depressing than *West of Suez,* Osborne's personal Waste Land beginning with a parody of antitheater—no plot or character, only improvisation—and having got that, with critics and audiences out of the way, he attacks other matters in a list so long that it excludes no one. The cast showed what virtuosity they could bring to the reading of a telephone directory. But here Bryden overlooks the way in which the long list that excludes no one is really (like the topics of Jimmy's anger in *Look Back*) a short list connecting sex, society, and language with the theater that should reflect them; and how that theater should and should not reflect them. Osborne-bashing was, as Sheridan Morley observed, a popular critical sport and *A Sense of Detachment,* like *Paul Slickey,* gave critics plenty of ammunition. But if the play was not *Hamlet* neither was it quite as bad as many insisted. The first half gives full rein to the old Osborne anger, starting from a simple question—What kind of play does an audience want?—which then widens to encompass "everything from the appalling nature of theater programs to the savagery of the American war effort." In the second half he gives us "a mixture of poetry, piety and porn" over which he bellows his final message to the 1970s: God rot you! But the theme that we no longer love merits attention and in this compendium of Osborne hatreds—"of his audience, his fellow-playwrights, this century and ultimately, one suspects, himself"—there is, surely, something for everyone.[8]

The End of Me Old Cigar

Pamela claims there is grace in detachment but in *A Sense of Detachment* Osborne was clearly not detached. To the relief of those, however, who like a plot and characters, Osborne returned to a kind of story in his next play, which opened at the Greenwich Theater on 16 January 1975. The venue was significant, marking Osborne's almost complete break with the Royal Court, whose decline he continues to describe with gusto:

To turn from the first 15 years of the Court to the present day is to lurch from the Rome of Augustus to that of Justinian, from the Republic of George and Tony to those barbarous, rapacious mercenaries, Ron and Les.[9]

The End of Me Old Cigar was written while he was working on another, more serious play, and is offered as a comedy:

I think it is simply funny but a lot of people find it objectionable. So what is comedy to me is a load of misery to a lot of other people. I thought *Look Back in Anger* was quite a comedy. But nobody else did. They thought it was a "Human Drama."[10]

The title, according to Osborne, comes from an old music-hall song that was a great favorite of Harry Champion and was quoted by Frank in *The Entertainer.*[11] Osborne calls the play "a modern comedy of manners" and it opens, appropriately, in a large country house, furnished extravagantly, full of mirrors, where the owner, Lady Regine Frimley, is listening to the final trio of *Der Rosenkavalier* (used previously in *A Sense of Detachment*). Her "husband," Stan—the sort of man who poses in the nude for magazines or manages pop groups or boutiques—is reading *Melody Maker* and the racing papers and has the trio explained to him: three women singing though one of them is supposed to be a man. Was it written by a man, he asks innocently? By two overbearing Viennese pigs, is Regine's tart reply as she launches into a seminar on Mozart, who really understood women and made all his men such fools. From this interpretation we move easily into an explanation of the setting. The house is a high-class brothel where, for some time, all the important men in England have been served, photographed by Stan. The evidence has been deposited in the bank, though rather carelessly in a joint account to which Regine has lost her key. Now the hour of revolution has come, the time when Ms. Lenin should arrive at the Finland Station, and Regine has sent for a hard-hitting female reporter, Stella Shrift, to whom she explains this situation. Lady Regine, née Myra Steinitz, a Jewish girl from Hackney, seems to have done well out of her husbands though her dislikes are legion. When she is asked if there is anything she does like, she rattles off a list that includes champagne, chip butties, Guinness, opera, Jane Austen (but not Conrad), silver rollerskating, and sex—now and then. She has miles of film which will make Watergate look like three-day cricket for baboons and she is preparing for the last weekend in this Garsington of Lechery. Her ladies begin to arrive (and some of the fun was trying to identify whom the author had in mind); they include, inevitably, a militant American academic Woman's Libber, Jog Fienberg—a "sperm vampire"—and Mrs. Isobel Sands. She is an unlikely member, but because Osborne needs her and Len Grimthorpe for act 2 a certain amount of time has to be spent trying to justify the presence of either in this remarkable establishment. This entails biographical details which have a deeper resonance than the glib but amusing biographies of the other characters, but the tone is, momentarily, spoiled. Isobel has been married nearly twenty years, has three teenage children who terrify both her and her husband, and has failed with him, too, reducing him to such despair that he dreads coming home. Len has decided not to be brilliant because he could not bear it and believes in the beauty of failure. He is quite harmless, dull, and "totally male" and Regine cannot think why she asked him since he is not really famous.

The arrival of two more ladies restores the tone and Regine's control over the scene and she launches into a splendid tirade which allows Osborne to give us a list of his dislikes. Isobel meets Len, and the two go off together. Act 1 has been almost completely aggressive, satirical, and amusing. But the Restoration romp falters and act 2 moves in another direction, the sentimental. As the other guests assemble they watch Isobel and Len through a two-way mirror and are disturbed to find that, after forty minutes, they still have their clothes on and are sitting on the bed "talking like two men in the Athenaeum."[12] The overworked joke about a man not being able to get it up puts an end to the scene, and scene 2 looks at the growing relationship between Isobel and Len as they discover that they love one another: desire will not fail even though they will make love with the lights on! Scene 3 confirms that they have achieved their vision. They are both contented "almost to the point of smugness" and we gather from references to the soreness of Fido that things went very well. Indeed, when Regine enters she says that they look as if they have had a vision. The other guests are leaving or have left and Regine is appalled to find that Stan has sold all the film records to Ashley Withers, the newspaper proprietor, for a large sum of money and now proposes to go and spend it in a villa in Spain with birds and everything. "Judas," the women cry out as they realize they will have to start from the beginning again, and Jog rather foolishly starts to quote from one of the great love tragedies, *Anthony and Cleopatra*.

Isobel completes the quotation and Len, recalling Kipling's "The Betrothed," reminds them: "At least in your cases: A WOMAN IS A WOMAN BUT A GOOD CIGAR IS A SMOKE."

Harold Hobson felt that there was a gleam of hope in this finely conceived play[13] though whether the hope was for England, now no longer a decaying music hall but a brothel run by female militants, or for Osborne the dramatist was unclear. What was clear was that the split between the two acts was fatal. Ivan Howlett, in *Plays and Players* (March 1975), observed that *Cigar* is a play that starts as one thing but ends as another. The first act starts as a Restoration satire and prepares us for "orgy and revolution in the second Act." But then Osborne ditches the satirical framework, axes characters who have just arrived, and finishes the play with a love scene between Keith Barron and Jill Bennett "with a haste that suggests either loss of interest or a need to take his typewriter for servicing." Commenting that these two are unlikely candidates for such a place and that their dialogue is improbable, Howlett concedes that Osborne can still thrill the auditor, particularly in Regine's outburst in act 1. The piece has an air of contemporaneity about it, with references to well-known figures in society, but it remains a revue rather than a play.

One could also object, apart from the shift in direction, that the plot is unconvincing. Who, in 1975, would be surprised at the kind of revelations Regine and her gang propose to make? But the improbable produces a splendid first act—Osborne has rarely written such funny dialogue—and the preoccupation with sex, money, and power puts the play in the tradition of Congreve and Wilde.

Watch It Come Down

Osborne wrote *The End of Me Old Cigar* while working on another, more serious play and this, presumably, was *Watch It Come Down,* published in 1975 but not staged until 24 February 1976 at the National Theater. This is the last stage play to date and represents a return to the group play: a man and his dependents in a particular crisis situation. Asked by Tynan what he would buy if he had unlimited money, Osborne said that he longed for space and would like "to live in a place as big as a railway station."[14] This group of characters do just that. A country railway station has been converted expensively, but not entirely successfully, into a fairly comfortable penthouse. Here Ben Prosser, who used to be a revolutionary young film director, uncorrupted by his Oscars but now in his mid-forties, has brought his novelist wife, Sally, her sister Shirley (who paints and attends protest rallies), Glen, an old homosexual friend (who is dying in the Parcels Office), Jo, who loves and looks after Glen, and Raymond, a "quiet, dog-of-all-work homosexual" in his late thirties. Upstairs there is Ben's mother with her cats and the television. Ben has been married before, to Marion, and has a daughter by that marriage. As the play opens Sally is asking Raymond what they are all doing here—the Prossers, tired of the Rat Race, when, she complains, she was just getting into her stride. And as for showing initiative by converting a railway station in the country they could, she observes, have had a Palladian gem for the money they have wasted on this rural folly. She tells Raymond that she and Ben are parting and asks him to tell their friends, dropping an odd hint when she remarks: "Should be interesting. Their concern, I mean."[15]

Ben returns from a disastrous lunch with his daughter and immediately he and Sally begin a fight during which other background details emerge. Ben's father (Welsh, of course) has just died and his funeral (all requiems, music-hall songs, boozing, and sponging) contrasts with what Sally's father would expect. He is in the Colonial Service. Thus Sally comes from the right background for country living since, as Glen observes later, the country is now the last outpost of Empire to which all the district officers have retired and who have no intention of handing over power again. Certainly the countryside around the station is seething with hatred and resentment as palpable as that from the darkness in *West of Suez*. Ben has just had a row with Major Bluenose over his dog (which will worry sheep) and the layabouts he keeps in the station. Ben finds that living in the country is very much an echo of memories of old India in *West of Suez*:

> All ex-housemasters, rear admirals, prying vicars, prowling group captains, ladies with walking sticks and scarves, tombola, pony events and the *Daily Telegraph*.[16]

Sally, who grew up in the country, cannot imagine why Ben thought it would be anything else. In the town people have to give way but the country is "not green much and rarely pleasant."

The news of the separation affects people differently; Glen is unperturbed as he finishes his book and prepares to die while Shirley bursts into tears. Ben blames the difficulty of living in the twentieth century, a loveless time and a loveless place. Sally, who has gone for a walk with the dog, enters with the dead dog, which has been shot after the countryfolk have set all their dogs on to it and raped it. Ben and Sally begin to fight in earnest now and, as Raymond stands holding the dead dog, they tear and smash one another and the station as the curtain falls.

A short second act brings it all down. Sally and Jo have a brief love idyll together until the doctor arrives. It then emerges that the separation was only a trial of their friends which Glen rightly thinks is disgusting. He also now sees that his life's work is useless and he dies, leaving a world that cannot understand the things that he believed in—the world of "Berenson down to Maugham via Cunard Junction." What, asks Sally, will life be like when he and his cultured kind disappear?

Meanwhile Ben's ex-wife, Marion, appears, Jo throws herself under the last train to pass through the station, and, as the doctor returns, the countryfolk start shooting up the station, Jo's dead body, and Ben, who collapses "clearly almost dead or in a coma." They do all, as the doctor says, lead odd lives—to which Sally says that he must be glad. But must we? Sally, unfortunately, in spite of her wit (she is another of those truthful monsters we should love) does not hold the play together. In act 2 Ben asks why it all has to be "so bad, so brutish, so devilish, so sneering?"[12] This could be applied to the play. The obvious points are all there—an exclusive set being destroyed between the new and the old world. But is it possible to care for this group? Alan Brien described them, in a long review in *Plays and Players* (April 1976), as

> an in-bred, anaemic coterie of refugees cut off from any interest in a real world of human splendors and miseries, hopes and fears, self-exiles in a dreary desert of selfishness.

Twenty years after the opening of the Royal Court Osborne, its first great critical and commercial success, was chosen as one of four living playwrights to open the National Theater and this, his twentieth play (give or take a TV play or filmscript) seemed, to Brien, an unhappy choice. The exposition, he points out, is as clumsy as the set (and that has to collapse every night). It is not even effectively informative since it is written in what might be called "that clotted cryptic shorthand, characteristic of middle period Osborne, somewhere between an epigram and a telegram." The play hardly improves as it goes on and remains, simply, an un-play, a "circular tour around the shrinking world of Paul Slickey, conducted by a dramatist . . . increasingly lost and adrift inside his own skull."

In one sense, certainly, the play does recall *Paul Slickey* and G. K. Hunter's criticism that "the world of Paul Slickey is too small, too parochial, too monomaniac to convey the important things that Osborne has to say."[18]

Chapter Eight
Odd Jobs

Although Osborne's experience in adapting Lope de Vega had not been particularly happy and although he continues to have a low opinion of television his work outside the theater after *The Hotel in Amsterdam* (1968) consists of three adaptations and no less than six plays for television.

Hedda Gabler

Hedda, like Leonido (and Coriolanus and Dorian Gray), is an outsider, and provided a splendid opportunity for Jill Bennett to whom the play is dedicated. It opened at the Royal Court on 28 June 1972 and a Yorkshire Television production was transmitted on 3 March 1981, with Diana Rigg playing the part of Hedda. For this severely abridged version of the play Osborne enlarged upon his introduction to the text published in 1972 where he declared a long-standing fascination with the play. In his article for the *TV Times* (28 February–9 March 1981) he also recalls the earlier article "Sex and Failure" (1957).

Apart from his usual criticism of television (which comes oddly from someone who has abridged his play for the medium) he complains of the prevailing fashion for plays not about human beings but about Problems. What is this play about and is it relevant? Hedda, he suggests, is not to be seen as unliberated woman or a marriage problem, nor is the play a vehicle for the resentments of the middle class against Society. *Hedda Gabler* is a rich play only if the heroine is taken in the context of the other characters. They are, in fact, a shabby lot and by comparison she at least has the "gift of energy." But Osborne also sees her as "petty, frigid and clearly unable to carry through any relationship significantly." She is bored but she chose to be bored. She has wit but no humor, and she has her fun at the expense of others. She must always be the center of attention and would like to be a great lady, but whatever she does or whatever happens to her she will be bored.[1]

Russell Davies, reviewing this sprint through the play in the *Sunday Times,* observed that there was little opposition to the "pantherish Rigg" and the camera kept going so merrily that her boredom hardly seemed appropriate or possible; but, as he suggests, "yawning Scandinavians don't sell dog food." Geoffrey Cannon, also in the *Sunday Times* (1 March 1981), remarked how typically Osborne the play was. The society in which Hedda lives was rendered so cursorily that her actions no longer seemed inevitable:

> she appears a bitch, and Hedda is not merely a bitch. The Osborne version . . . has turned Ibsen's tragedy into a study in cynicism.

But Irving Wardle, in *The Times* (30 June 1972), called the original stage production "a faithful version" while John Mortimer saw the play stripped of literary trimmings allowing us to feel it with a fresh emotional impact.[2] Any judgment of the adaptation rests on two bases: one's view of translation and one's view of Hedda. Sheridan Morley conceded that the cobwebs had been blown off the play but was unable to find any indication that a playwright rather than a mere translator had been at work. Here we get nothing more than "an efficient trip through the plot."[3] His view that Jill Bennett was "oddly lightweight" should, however, have alerted him to what Osborne's thesis was: *Hedda Gabler* is not a one-woman play and Hedda is petty, bored, frigid, and a born loser. This is not everyone's view of her, of course. Irma Kurtz, in *Plays and Players* (August 1972), sees Hedda as "trapped Everywoman." Osborne, she felt, in trying to make everything plausible to a modern audience, has diminished Hedda. Burning Lovborg's manuscript becomes headstrong jealousy rather than self-destruction, and Judge Brack's villainy seems "more goose-feather than the straw that breaks Hedda's last hope and sends her off into a rather high-spirited suicide." Ibsen's Hedda, "stifling under middle-class morality, choking on her own taste and talent," could shoot herself, but not "hysterics like Osborne's Hedda who are fuelled by vanity."

A Place Calling Itself Rome

In an interview for the *Observer* (30 June 1968) Osborne remarked that he had abandoned a project to rewrite *Coriolanus* set in an African republic because he did not know whether he wanted "to write a play about public feeling when all my instincts were focussing down on interior things and people's inner self." *A Place Calling Itself Rome* was published in 1973 and has, so far, never been staged. As the title says, the action still takes place in Rome but the adaptation offers parallels with modern politics and contemporary life. Bernard Shaw described *Coriolanus* as Shakespeare's finest comedy—and it is certainly, with the great tragedies in mind—a difficult play. North's Plutarch describes Coriolanus as brave and noble but "for lack of education" so choleric and impatient "that he would yield to no living creature." Coriolanus strives to be heroic but it is a self-destructive quality because it lacks that other side of greatness, the ability to live with other people. Shakespeare sets his solitary man in a complex social system. Shakespeare's view of the crowd is not flattering but they are not shown as unintelligent. They can be easily lead by the self-seeking Tribunes but they are part of the state, and their fickleness is as bad for that state as the fixity of Coriolanus. The hero's solitude is emphasized at the end of the play when Aufidius insults him, calling forth from Coriolanus the memorable line, "Alone I did it."

This angry, superior young man, with an awful mother, was obviously congenial to Osborne. The text has no introductory note and the adaptation, if we compare scene by scene, is fairly straightforward. The title—*A Place Calling Itself Rome*—suggests that we may apply the lessons wherever they fit and is in many ways more suitable for Shakespeare's version. *Coriolanus* is first and foremost about Rome, whereas Osborne's version looks more deeply into the personality of the hero. Thus Osborne invents a first scene in the bedroom of Coriolanus as he dreams (recalling the opening scenes of *Inadmissible Evidence* and *A Patriot for Me*). In his loss of concentration, inability to sleep or make decisions and the recognition that both sex and speech are failing him Coriolanus reminds us of Maitland. The troubled nature of the hero, then, and his problem of reconciling private feeling with the public voice that the people expect from him, precedes our introduction to the crowd with which Shakespeare opens his play. Osborne's crowd is composed of the usual Rent-A-Mob characters and the fable of the belly preached by Menenius is replaced by the riddle of Change—a political speech soothing the mob until the arrival of Coriolanus. His first comment on the mob is that they have no laughter in them. They are frightened by peace and war, they have neither pride nor fear. When Menenius speaks of their demands Coriolanus asks what they are offering to the state, but Menenius can only couch these offers in the jargon of "industrial relations. Conformist ideals; technocratic skills, prevailing ideologies. . . ."[4] The Tribunes of the people arrive. Osborne has turned Sicinius into a "pale-skinned colored woman" who comes in last, making, as Coriolanus notes, the kind of theatrical gesture he expects from her. News of the Volsces closes the scene.

Osborne keeps the scenes short, briskly introducing us to Aufidius in Corioli, Coriolanus's mother and his wife, Virgilia, who is given more of a character than she has in Shakespeare. The battle scenes are reduced in number but not in scope since they are waged with armored vehicles, parachutists, and all the paraphernalia of modern mechanized warfare. Coriolanus arrives home at a modern airport and the Tribunes plot in a conference room. Osborne naturally expands the role of the Tribunes and emphasizes both their self-interest and their lack of insight. When Coriolanus is proposed for consul Osborne replaces the speech of Cominius which celebrates the deeds of the hero with a short speech commenting on the ignorance of the people who must vote but whose ignorance makes greatness an alien quantity. Coriolanus, thinking of the nightmare in act 1, scene 1, cannot speak to the people in the manner they expect—the everyday coinage, as Menenius calls it. He does, however, attempt the public voice and gains the vote. Osborne removes much of the sympathy Shakespeare allows the crowd until the Tribunes begin to manipulate it, and he makes the objections of Coriolanus clearer. How can you satisfy the Siciniuses of Rome who say:

> "We are the strongest because we are the most, to hell with the best . . . What we make, we shall *employ*." Not invent, mark you. . . .[5]

Osborne moves with speed through the mob scene to the banishment scene, creating a strong sense both of urgency and of the conspiracy on the part of the Tribunes.

Act 2 begins at the airport with the departure of Coriolanus and moves rapidly in ten short scenes through acts 4 and 5 of Shakespeare's play: the Tribunes smug in their triumph, Coriolanus in a pub at Antium, the meeting with Aufidius where Osborne inserts into the speech in which Coriolanus tells Aufidius either to kill him or use him, the telling phrase: "Even *you* might do with *my* spleen."[6] Back in Rome the Tribunes close the file on Coriolanus (it is marked "rendered harmless") as the news of the joint attack on the city begins to filter through. Various emissaries are sent out and his mother succeeds in changing Coriolanus (thus fueling the professional jealousy of Aufidius who, in scene 6, sounds very like the Tribunes). Aufidius denounces Coriolanus, who has a speech not in Shakespeare on the nature of patriotism. Aufidius is a true patriot and a good hater but his hatred is vulnerable to self-interest because it is not thought out. The Volscians are like the Romans: everything by starts and nothing long. The conspirators murder Coriolanus and Aufidius can regret his passing because he stood for something constant: ". . . neither to change, nor falter, nor repent even this . . . to him was to be good, great and joyous, beautiful. . . ."[7] But where Shakespeare can allow his hero a noble memory the modern Coriolanus has, as his epitaph, only the possibility that "someone may remember." A helicopter raises the body as the stage empties, leaving a lone piper to play a lament.

The devices and tone of the play obviously recall Brecht, but here Brechtian means much the same as Shakespearean. Brecht, whose own adaptation of *Coriolanus* was written about 1951–53 and produced in 1962 (by the Berliner Ensemble in 1964), found the Elizabethan theater ideal for the expression of Marxist dialectic since it was cumulative rather than conclusive. And Brecht noted that Shakespeare could present events, relations, and actions of a contradictory kind all in one scene, which was rare in bourgeois theater.

The Picture of Dorian Gray

Described as "A Moral Entertainment" this adaptation of the novel by Oscar Wilde was written in 1972, published in 1973, and staged at the Greenwich Theater on 13 February 1975. In his introduction Osborne asks the questions: why? how? By the end of his note we have some impressions but no clear answer. He confesses that he likes the novel in spite of its melodramatic qualities because he has "always admired over-bold gestures in the service of style in writing and in everything else"[8] and his introduction is a series of gestures on a "take-it-or-leave it" basis. He connects the novel with Stevenson's *Dr. Jekyll and Mr. Hyde* and sees it as a variation on the Faustian pact. But ideas are two a penny: "Execution is all, which as the programmers of Television Companies never seem to realise, is a very different thing from 'packaging.' "[9] What struck him about the original was its "feeling of wilful courage and despair" and the subject matter: youth and beauty. The Victorians thought this bargain with the Devil not merely wicked but bizarre since it went against nature but today the pursuit of youth and beauty is all important and youth is all powerful.

If execution is all, what then has Osborne done with the Wilde novel? For the most part he has sewn together dialogue from the twenty chapters into thirteen scenes. Thus act 1 covers the first seven chapters: the portrait is finished, Dorian's wish is expressed, he meets Lord Henry, falls in love with Sibyl, rejects her, and notices the first change in the portrait. Act 2 draws into one scene material from chapters 8 through 19, though Osborne has Dorian send a note to Sibyl before Lord Henry arrives with news of her suicide, and where, in Wilde, Basil Hallward visits Dorian after the opera, in Osborne that visit precedes the opera. Act 3, scene 1 shows Osborne covering much of the ground in chapters 11 through 13. The stage is peopled with characters who have appeared earlier in the story and who show how time has changed them. The twenty years, however, have made no difference to Dorian and in a long speech he covers the action of those intervening years and gets into the play, rather well, the long section on Dorian's hedonism and hobbies—collecting vestments, perfumes, music, jewels—filling in the background until the arrival of Hallward, who is shown the picture and murdered. Scene 2 covers the meeting with Allan Campbell while scene 3 makes a reference to Adrian Singleton but is used for the meeting with James Vane. But the young sailor is not told that Dorian has been young for twenty years and could have caused Sibyl's death and he neither peers through the conservatory window at Selby nor gets shot. In scene 4 Osborne uses the actress who played Sibyl to play the Dutchess of Monmouth but beyond that Dorian's faint is unmotivated. Scene 5 covers the episode in which Dorian gives up Hetty, the innocent country girl. In the final scene Osborne asks for lighting—"the nineteenth century version of a strobe pop scene"—and fills the air with music, shouts, screams, and moans. Dorian enters, stabs the portrait, and collapses. Two constables enter, flashing their lamps over the darkened room, where they discover "the remains of the portrait" and the "old carcass" of Dorian Gray. This is less successful than Wilde's chilling conclusion where the picture of Dorian Gray "in all the wonder of his exquisite youth and beauty" hangs above a withered corpse with a knife in his heart.

Despite the throw-away style of the introduction there are clues to what is happening. Osborne speaks of the infuriating nature of the original, deadly serious "when it should be self-mocking," and of the use of a woman to play the main role, which would produce an ambiguity and allow that part to be played straightforwardly, if ironically, and "defuse the camp period acting." We are to see the moral of the play as an attack on youth, selfishness, and the liberal conscience of today that answers evil with cults, occult sciences, and astrology—which can hardly explain the modern world of Charles Manson, hijackings, killing, bombings, and the "growing sophistication of horrors."

In his preface Wilde observes that there is no such thing as a moral or an immoral book: books are well written, or badly written. Presumably Osborne's "Execution is all" means something similar, so how well has he dramatized the tale? In chapter 2 of the novel Lady Agatha complains that the men argue and she can never make out what they are talking about. In fact the men do not argue, they merely exchange witty remarks. This works quite well in a novel, though even there the cleverness can grow wearisome, but in drama the absence of action, even the activity of discussion, is fatal. It is not really surprising that Wilde succeeded completely in only one of his nine plays. As John Lahr comments, in *Plays and Players* (April 1975), epigrams "are dramatic events on the page, but on the stage they pall without the counterpoint of action." We would not expect enthusiasm from Lahr, whose view of Osborne is not overgenerous, but here Osborne plays into his hands. Lahr pins down what is wrong with this very close adaptation. He points out that Dorian's corruption should be a more active event and clearly connected with the homosexual world which convention forced Wilde to disguise as offstage decadence. Lahr finds it ironic that Osborne, whose caricatures of homosexuals have been "as brutal and insensitive as exist in contemporary drama," should choose a novel whose energy comes from the homosexual experience. Osborne avoids the problem by not facing it!

Lahr's view of Osborne's treatment of homosexuality is, like everything else, contentious. It was precisely because Osborne had shown some insight into the problem that one came to the adaptation hoping for more than one gets. The implications are as murky and gift-wrapped as they are in Wilde, who indeed provides most of the wrapping. All adaptations present problems of judgment and this one most acutely. As Michael Anderson points out, Osborne rarely gives the impression of using another writer as a starting point for his own creativity: ". . . he appears rather to seize on certain obvious parallels with his own artistic interests and to exploit them with little of his customary linguistic vitality."[10] The protagonists may be very like Osborne heroes but it is a pity, perhaps, that Osborne should spend his time remaking them. It is true that his contemporaries were doing the same thing; where Osborne adapts Shakespeare, Ibsen, and Wilde, Wesker was adapting Shakespeare and Dostoevsky while Pinter, in his film scripts, has adapted a wide range of authors, including Proust. It may also be true (but it is doubtful) that, as John Russell Taylor suggests, such reworkings show "that Osborne is taking a new practical interest in his craft as such, the how as well as the why of what he was saying."[11]

Plays for Television

In 1961 Osborne complained that television was boring because it "*reduces* life and the human spirit" and twenty years later he is still describing plays for television as "just dramatized journalism about inadequacy or anorexia in high-rise flats or one-parent families in inner cities."[12] He was also explaining how he used the television play: "I just do the odd one occasionally when I get a one-shot idea. That's all TV can handle. It's comparable to short stories. And people seldom remember them."[13] Since 1970 Osborne has written six short stories.

The Right Prospectus

The Right Prospectus was transmitted by BBC 1 on 22 October 1970 and published the same year. James and Pauline Newbold, a young-to-middle-aged, childless couple are looking at various public schools. They reject the obvious choices like Eton and Harrow but they do not want one of the modern coeducational kind either. They settle on Crampton as a kind of in-between, where they will be "free and easy, but enclosed, but not harried or got at," where they can take advantage of time to read, think, make friends, play games, and sleep soundly afterwards.[14] Having chosen Crampton they enroll themselves and Osborne's note asks that no one should take any notice of the age, sex, or relations of the Newbolds: they are just new boys.[15] This is disturbing since by the time they do enroll Mrs. Newbold is visibly pregnant and as term passes this becomes more obvious to us and Newbold, who sees and thinks of her sexually, as his wife, all the time. For him, as he suspected from the beginning, the idea was a mistake. He comes from a working-class background and never went to University whereas his wife, who comes from a family bred in public schools, settles down quite happily and successfully. She even weeps at having to leave when term ends. Newbold cannot fit in, however, and makes only one friend, Partridge, another outsider sent here by his stepmother from a school where one could do what one liked and was coeducational and somehow unreal: like playing at not being at school. When Newbold leaves, Partridge watches from a distance so Newbold cannot even feel that he gained one friend from the experience. At the center of the play is the head boy of Newbold's house, Heffer, who explains the system to the puzzled Newbold:

> It's a daft system, the whole thing but so is the Divine Bloody Office, *and* the democratic process . . . the technological revolution where even the tin-openers don't work let alone the money system and workers and industry and the thoughts of Chairman bloody Mao.[16]

Newbold tries to adjust but, like patriotism, trying is not enough.[17]

Stanley Price, in *Plays and Players* (December 1970), thought that the play started off with a splendid idea but then "went absolutely nowhere and had absolutely nothing to say at considerable length" while Chris Dunkley, in *The Times*, found no central focus which left the play, for him, skipping about from one object of disgust to another.[18] Harold Ferrar, on the other hand, saw it as witty, if unchallenging, entertainment and suggested that one had to go back as far as *Under Plain Cover* to find a similar playfulness.[19] Katharine Worth got it right when she agreed that this was a little piece that came over as faintly comical but also, she noted, "faintly disturbing too." While his wife is a brilliant success Newbold seems trapped "in something more permanent than a dream."[20] The basic idea of using a particular focus to look at how society molds us and works—as in *Gulliver's Travels* or *The Way of All Flesh*—recurs in *Jill and Jack.*

Jill and Jack

Published with *The End of Me Old Cigar* in 1975, *Jill and Jack* was transmitted by Yorkshire Television on 11 September 1974. Again, the title and Osborne's note suggest how he uses the literal eye of the television camera to create a disturbing effect. There must, he insists, be no hint of homosexuality in the play: "They are very much two chaps and two girls. It is merely that their social roles have become rather confused, if not completely reversed."[21] Given this simple twist, the play is a straightforward account of an evening in the lives of Jill and Jack. Jill, a successful businesswoman, returns after a hard day at the office to her early nineteenth-century house in an attractive London square which she shares with Mary. With great efficiency she gets ready to take Jack to her club (which has bowed to progress and now allows men in on Thursday evenings and at Sunday lunch). Jack, a not-very-successful actor and model, gets ready with the help of his flat-mate, Mark, and is assisted on to the train by a porter, offered a seat by a young girl, throws his contraceptives away (something that can be left to her!), cannot find his ticket, and worries about the rain because he has just been to the crimpers, takes hours in the cloakroom, insists he is boring and ignorant about wine, and is taken aback when Jill proposes marriage. This will mean giving up his freedom, his flat with Mark, and looking after the children (and their nannies); he decides not to stay the night since he is having one of his odd turns. Mary returns after he has gone and the two girls settle down, thankfully, without men. Who needs them? They are poor at sex and have no inner life. The world in which all this takes place remains ordinary—that is, chauffeurs, porters, policemen, waiters are men where they usually are, reminding us constantly of the central confusion. There is also a parrot, Willie, who repeats crucial phrases but who, like all men, can be silenced without difficulty.

Matter of England

Osborne's England and his sense of patriotism are, not surprisingly, private matters. When Tynan asked him in 1968 if he was a patriot he replied that he was a patriot "in the sense that my life only has meaning here, not somewhere else."[22] Osborne's England, too, as Michael Anderson has pointed out, is less an historical reality than an imagined landscape, a kind of club whose members have proved that they can suffer and articulate that suffering. Tolerance is not a requirement:

> one consistent feature in Osborne's plays is . . . that contemporary society is suffering from a degeneration of feeling and language, and the hero's isolation becomes increasingly an impatient and wholesale rejection of modern times.[23]

Osborne has written two plays for television which reflect the disillusionment, boredom, and failure of approaching middle age: *Very Like a Whale* is the first. Published in 1971 (the year of *West of Suez*) it was not transmitted until 13 February 1980 by ATV. Bill Maitland collapsed under the weight of failure but Jock Mellor, played by Alan Bates, appears to be a great success. At the beginning of the play he is about forty-four and knighted by the queen for services to exports. As the play proceeds, however, we see him dissatisfied at work and at home, no longer willing to pretend, bored, sleeping badly, out of touch with his wife and daughter, his first wife and son (who live in America), his sister (married to an academic at Cambridge), and his father, who prefers the company of his television and dog. He lives in the usual Osborne world—London overrun by tourists, Americans, a lady journalist—and seems unable to keep any relationships, with his doctor or even with his old school chum, Stephen. Stephen is an artist who claims that he has marked out a small area of life which is private and which he can run as he likes, but while he says this his students are systematically vandalizing Jock's car in the street outside. Jock moves inexorably toward collapse and a death that goes almost unnoticed and unmourned. How, he asks, can one avoid cruelty and survive in the present time, which is so out of joint? Apart from an allusion to *Hamlet* in the title, Jock keeps remembering Cromwell, that chief of men, who raised the prestige of England abroad to a level unparalleled since the time of Elizabeth I. The star speaker at a Trade Conference argues that the unpleasant aspects of technology are not because there is a lack of control. Modern techniques are exercises in compromise: one cannot have the convenience and complain about the disadvantages. Jock agrees that may be so but deplores the fact that people will not face up to the truth, that they have made a slum into a desert in a present that is quite unthinkable. Success as failure recalls previous plays or, say, Pinter's *Tea Party* (1965), though Osborne's treatment lacks the obliqueness of the Pinter play. But Pinter's breakdown is personal and private where Osborne takes us out into a world of sullen workers, tourists, businessmen and air travelers. The link with the main body of Osborne's work is there, as Anderson observes, "in its impatience with the glibly patriotic self-justification of the industrial world, its anti-Americanism and its sense that the best of England's life is over."[24]

Geoffrey Cannon, in the *Sunday Times* (10 February 1980), saw the idea of a deracinated industrialist getting a knighthood on top of his riches as only the ostensible theme. Pointing out that Mellor sees himself in mirrors and the world through car or plane windows, that women are vampires or leeches, and that Britain is infested by vandals and run by men of unearned privilege, Osborne was saying: "women are like this, men are like this, the world now is like this. The ceremonies and transactions in the play have no meaning." Jock remarks that this is not an age for friendship, and *The Gift of Friendship*, published in 1972, reflects a similar concern for English civilization, language, and style, and the same disgust and boredom with the present day.

The Gift of Friendship

Jocelyn Broome, an eminent writer in his early fifties, invites an old acquaintance, Bill Wakely, to dinner after a gap of ten years. They are both writers and share a common background though their paths diverged very early. Jocelyn was in the war (India, elephants, and sepoys) while Bill stayed at home and edited a literary journal. This, in itself, is not a dividing factor for, as Jocelyn says, patriotism, like honor, is one's own business. What divides them is integrity since Bill is little more than a "sort of cultural travelling salesman." His life-style, his wives, are all part of this but Jocelyn knows that he will come to dinner even if his latest wife is not invited because he has curiosity. Madge, his latest wife, does disapprove and Bill does visit Jocelyn, where he is surprised to find that Jocelyn wants him to be his literary executor. Jocelyn says that this should protect his work from the American universities and their endless exegesis. As Broome sees it writers have failed: we had the finest language in the world and a civilization to match—captured in the play by recollections and photographs—and now we see England being turned into a strip of concrete and a rumbling stench. In Wakely's world Judas becomes "an idealistic pop plugger worried about his boy" in a "mind-busting number called Gethsemane."[25] And both Madge and Bill burn a Broome first edition—though Bill's fire is an accident. Broome is troubled, too, by the elusive nature of inspiration—like mining, a matter of investment until the seam runs out.

After his death Bill and Madge, reading his obituary, discuss the relationship between Bill and Jocelyn. Neither liked the other but, as Madge points out, Jocelyn was himself: "He went his own funny little way."[28] When Bill collects the Broome papers he discovered how much Broome hated him and his world:

There are only two finalities . . . Hell and America. The United States and Despair. What a shabby little creature Wakely is. Fawning on everyone because he is so scared—no, in anguish, at the idea of being left out or ignored.[27]

Bill is genuinely surprised that he could be hated but he will not send the papers to an American university: Broome had made his wishes pretty clear. Madge observes that if Bill can do the same when he dies he will have done pretty well!

What is interesting in this slight play is that none of the characters is contemptible. Madge, Bill's wife, seems bitchy and is certainly vindictive in the book-burning scene, but she emerges at the end of the play as a woman of perception with a neat way of putting things. Bill survives the gift of friendship and is better for it. The absence of asperity and a certain mellowness of tone were both pleasing and hopeful, and both are continued in the two plays published in 1978.

You're Not Watching Me, Mummy

Yorkshire Television was to transmit this play on 30 July 1979 but, because of industrial action, transmission was postponed until 20 January 1980. *You're Not Watching Me, Mummy* opens with shots of Shaftesbury Avenue, awash with "the moving garbage of modern tourism" while a voice-over intones clichés about inflation, no man is an island, and every visitor is now a Londoner because what counts is the money he brings. The action then moves into one of the theaters, to the star's dressing room, where Jemima (b. 1932, in Nairobi) and her homosexual dresser, Leslie, predict who will come in after the show for free drinks. The list is long and gives Osborne plenty of opportunities to introduce his favorite targets and, as they chatter, his favorite themes. There is the Marxist Women's Lib author who laughs too loudly at her own play; Stanley Klob, a research student from Seattle; the girl who will do anything to become an actress; an old school-chum and her husband (who refer to one another as Boot and Petal); Susan, divorced that very day from Jemima's ex-husband, and her latest escort, Anthony, the gay friend who has problems and a new Sealyham; Frederic Lamont, critic and Jemima's biographer (with a withered arm); and many more. Jemima, after working hard for two and a half hours, just wants to get home to a cup of Ovaltine and her bed: which she does, slipping away almost unnoticed. But who cares?

The situation, if slight, is suitable for television and suits Osborne. He likes his two main characters, who have long standing rapport; the play is witty, making its points sardonically; and the tone is mellow. Much of this, unfortunately, was lost in transmission. It was a plodding production, the camera work was unbelievably clumsy, there was an unfortunate break for the commercial, and Anna Massey, as Jemima, did not bring to the role the cheerful malice Jill Bennett would have given it. It was altogether, after so long a wait, disappointing and lackluster—and Osborne, of course, got the credit. Russell Davies, in the *Sunday Times,* saw it as the sort of play anyone locked up with a typewriter could produce about a theater dressing room and here Osborne gave us "a loud parade of our preconceptions."[28] Michael Church, in *The Times*, felt that the question was no longer whether Osborne was a major dramatist or not, but whether he was a dramatist at all:

> Contemporary Britain is despatched by means of jaundiced generalizations delivered on behalf of the author. There is an underlying thread of pathos. The plot is of the slimmest.

He allows that the relationship between Jemima and Leslie ("one of desperate mutal need") works but he feels that dramatizing boredom is something Osborne cannot do, while the language "of the kind which used to be called 'basic' but which now sound pathetically dated" grated on his ear. What was dated was this review: 19 January 1980. Critics now review Osborne before we can even see the show.

Try a Little Tenderness

You're Not Watching Me, Mummy required a great deal of style; *Try a Little Tenderness* also requires considerable resources and would be a daunting task for a television production. The one-shot idea is the reactions in a village to the arrival of a pop festival, with strong echoes of *Watch It Come Down*. The large number of targets and themes is organized around Ted Shilling, a writer in his fifties from a working-class background who is successful enough to retire to the country although his work, at the moment, lacks something. In Arkley, where the old brigade resent his arrival, he lives with his dog, Colditz; his wife, an ex-ballet dancer, who is bored with living in a rural slum and imports as much of the Covent Garden atmosphere and people as she can; his mother-in-law, who is constantly recalling the good old days in Hong Kong; and his son, Robert, who has brought his girl friend, Slim, and other friends to squat in part of the house. Ted pays for, cooks for, waits on, and puts up with all these—his only pleasure being his dog and his relationship with Slim. The villagers think of him as a patient man who puts up with too much but he replies:

I just know how to wait and when to strike—it's the heart beat of all art. It's my mother-in-law's eighty-ninth birthday today . . . I think certain special occasions are good for making fresh decisions.[29]

The coincidence of the birthday, the pop festival, and a new mistress brings about those decisions. He organizes the villagers to fight the pop festival, whose participants stream into the village by the thousand, returns home to settle his wife and her friends (by shoving the chocolate cake into the face of one of those friends), plants drugs among the squatters, phones the police, and then settles down with Slim to watch the attack on the festival—with sheep, cows, farm machinery, the full splendors of the hunt, and over all the church bells which used to infuriate Jimmy Porter! The battle of Arkley, however, soon ceases to be Ealing comedy as the various animals, machines, and people tangle and panic. When Ted is asked if he is satisfied he replies, "No, but I never expected to be." As he walks away with Slim the camera moves into an aerial view of the countryside; which is where the play began.

Ted is a resourceful character with a good sense of timing; the music in the play adds to our sense of his sense of what is appropriate. When dealing with his mother-in-law he hums "On the Road to Mandalay," when planting drugs it is "Smoke Gets in Your Eyes," and with his wife he whistles the song that gives the play its title: "Try a Little Tenderness." At the beginning of the play he is told he should defend his rights, stand up and be counted. But, he asks, who with?

Chapter Nine
A Talent to Vex

If Osborne were asked whether or not he was satisfied I suspect his answer might be: No, but I never expected to be. And the critic who is not a hagiographer will not be satisfied either, though some conclusions can be drawn.

Public Voice, Private Feeling

When Harold Hobson detected two voices in *Look Back*—one noisy, the other quiet—he suggested a duality explored by many critics subsequently, a duality which seemed to pull Osborne in two different directions: Public Voice and Private Feeling. It was a useful critical tool but it fostered the idea that Osborne wrote two kinds of play—a personal drama or a social statement—and that the two rarely fuse into an artistic whole.

Although Osborne had been careful to state his aims and methods in 1957 and insisted that he would fulfill these as a dramatist rather than a Socialist or a teacher he has still been seen as either slipshod in his treatment of social themes (and compared, unfavorably, with Shaw) or as interested only in brilliant performances (and therefore important for the theater regardless of his qualities as a dramatist). This "problem" of how far Osborne is or is not a committed dramatist has intensified as the years have gone by and as his characters grow richer and more socially successful and the language of anger gives way to petulance.

Osborne unquestionably has a way with words—"our last link with God," as he puts it[1]—but many critics find he does not make them work. Osborne is personally aware that the theater today is fragmented, its audience sharing nothing "but the climate of dissociation in which it tries to live its baffled lives." What remains for him, then, is to be "specific to himself and his own particular, concrete experience."[2] And in doing this he has reached a wider audience than might seem possible today.

The Misanthropist

But is his appeal more than what John Whiting called "the universal appeal of misanthropy"?[3] His dislike of critics is understandable: they should have been there to help the audience assimilate his lessons in feeling. But the essay on "Critics and Criticism" (1961) was light in tone; telegrams of anger after *A Bond Honoured* are no substitute. And the proposal, in 1977, to form an authors' Mafia and select a critic for physical assault might be seen as a gesture to rouse England from its torpor, but it would have come better from a dramatist producing work of the highest caliber!

Because his work is so varied and instinctive he is a difficult dramatist to deal with. Love, death, and betrayal are hard topics to write about in the cool of the study. But when John Lahr complains of suffocation in the later works he misses the point. Coward rightly detected vitality, not anger, in Osborne's first success, and vitality diminishes. Maitland laments that his facility to assimilate things is failing—the halfway stage between the young man in *Look Back* who could grab anything and use it and the apprehensive conjuror in *The Hotel in Amsterdam* who puts out his hand into the void, uncertain of inspiration.

"Peppered with Comedy"

Osborne, like George Dillon, attracts hostility. The theater itself was Osborne's brave good cause, the middle class his enemy. They must be made to feel (which in England requires extraordinary effort), and, as time passed, other enemies were added to the list. But the real enemy, as Gabriel Gersh points out, was always the common man who allows critics, press, and Royal Family their stupid power.[4]

Like Shaw Osborne had to use a lot of "Laughing Gas." Everything he writes he sees as "peppered with comedy" but he no longer knows where he could send a play if he were to write one and he feels restricted by dialogue.[5] He has published the first volume of his autobiography and thinks he might write novels in his old age.[6] *A Better Class of Person* is, of course, as much a performance as any of his plays and quite the best thing he has written since *Inadmissible Evidence*. It shows admirable control over words, tone, and feelings, evokes an era and a class, and is rich in comedy and source material for the plays. It ends in 1956, apparently to prevent legal action from the Royal Court, which shows that Osborne still has a talent to abuse.

Notes and References

Preface

1. Simon Trussler, *The Plays of John Osborne* (London, 1969), p. 13.
2. Ibid., pp. 16, 17.

Chapter One

1. *A Better Class of Person: An Autobiography: 1929–1956* (London and Boston, 1981), p. 54.
2. Michael Billington, *The Modern Actor* (London, 1973), pp. 162–63.
3. "That Awful Museum," reprinted in *John Osborne: Look Back in Anger: A Casebook,* ed. John Russell Taylor (London, 1968), p. 66; hereafter cited as *Casebook.*
4. *Observer*, 18 November 1979.
5. Quoted in Martin Banham, *Osborne* (Edinburgh, 1969), p. 100.
6. Quoted in Richard Findlater, *Theatrical Censorship in Britain* (London: MacGibbon & Kee, 1967; Panther edition, 1968), pp. 213–14.
7. Quoted in Banham, *Osborne*, p. 100.
8. "That Awful Museum," p. 66.
9. Osborne's refusal to contribute to Irving Wardle's study *The Theatres of George Devine* (London: Jonathan Cape, 1978) is unfortunate for us but his reason, the private nature of his ten-year relationship with Devine, must be respected. Some inkling of his feeling comes through in "On the Writer's Side," in *At The Royal Court: 25 Years of the English Stage Company,* ed. Richard Findlater (Derbyshire, 1981), pp. 19–26.
10. See Wardle, *Theatres of Devine*; Terry Browne, *Playwrights' Theatre* (London: Pitman Publishing, 1975); *At the Royal Court*, ed. Findlater; and John Russell Taylor, "Ten Years of the English Stage Company," and Gordon Rogoff, "Richard's Himself Again," both in *British Theatre: 1956–1966, Tulane Drama Review,* no. 34 (Winter 1966), pp. 120–31, 29–40.
11. During the Vedrenne-Barker regime at the Court (1904–7), of the thirty-two plays performed eleven were by Shaw. Galsworthy's first play, *The Silver Box,* was accepted immediately and during these three years the Court also performed plays by Yeats, Housman, Maeterlinck, and Schnitzler.
12. *Sunday Times,* 1 March 1981.
13. Ibid.
14. Rogoff, "Richard's Himself," p. 33.
15. Quoted in Sheridan Morley, *A Talent to Amuse* (Harmondsworth: Penguin, 1974), p. 345.

16. Wardle, *Theatres of Devine,* p. 181.
17. "That Awful Museum," pp. 66, 67.
18. *Sunday Times,* 24 November 1974.
19. Kenneth Tynan, *A View of the English Stage* (Frogmore, 1976), p. 175.
20. "They Call It Cricket," in *Declaration,* ed. Tom Maschler (London: MacGibbon & Kee, 1957), p. 81.
21. Allardyce Nicoll, "Somewhat in a New Dimension," *Contemporary Theatre,* ed. J. R. Brown and B. Harris (London, 1962), pp. 77–95.
22. Wardle, *Theatres of Devine,* p. 183.
23. *Casebook,* p. 192.
24. Wilson Knight, "The Kitchen Sink," *Encounter* 21, no. 6 (December 1963):50.
25. Gareth Lloyd Evans, *The Language of Modern Drama* (London, 1977), p. 106.
26. John Russell Brown, *Theatre Language* (London, 1972), p. 131.
27. Ronald Hayman, *British Theatre Since 1955: A Reassessment* (Oxford, 1979), p. 10.
28. Trussler, *Plays of Osborne,* p. 55.
29. Morley, *Talent to Amuse,* p. 350.
30. *Casebook,* p. 12.
31. *Protest,* ed. Gene Feldman and Max Gartenberg (New York: Citadel, 1958; London: Souvenir Press, 1959), p. 12.
32. See, however, Kenneth Tynan, "The Angry Young Movement," *Tynan on Theatre* (Harmondsworth, 1964), pp. 54–62; John Holloway, "Tank in the Stalls: Notes on the 'School of Anger,' " *Hudson Review* 10 (1957–58):424–29; and Carl Bode, "The Redbrick Cinderellas," *College English* 20, no. 7 (1959):331–37.
33. Laurence Kitchin, *Mid-Century Drama* (London: Faber, 1960), p. 100.
34. Banham, *Osborne,* p. 2.
35. Katharine J. Worth, "The Angry Young Man: John Osborne," in *Experimental Drama,* ed. William A. Armstrong (London, 1963), p. 149.
36. Harold Ferrar, *John Osborne* (New York, 1973), p. 11.
37. "They Call It Cricket," p. 84.
38. John Mander, *The Writer and Commitment* (London, 1961), p. 22.
39. Ibid., pp. 187–88.
40. Edwin Morgan, "That Uncertain Feeling," in *Encore Reader* (London: Methuen & Co., 1965), p. 53.
41. Rogoff, "Richard's Himself," pp. 30–31.
42. *Declaration,* p. 65.
43. Introduction to *International Theatre Annual, Number Two,* ed. Harold Hobson (London: Calder, 1957), pp. 9, 10.

44. *Casebook,* p. 61.
45. "They Call It Cricket," pp. 83–84.
46. *Observer,* 7 July 1968.
47. *Sunday Times,* 1 March 1981.
48. *A Better Class of Person,* p. 23.
49. *Look Back in Anger* (London, 1957), pp. 9–10.
50. Ibid., p. 15.
51. Ibid., p. 17.
52. Trussler, *Plays of Osborne,* p. 45.
53. *Look Back in Anger,* p. 37.
54. Ibid., pp. 39, 40.
55. Trussler, *Plays of Osborne,* p. 50.
56. *Look Back in Anger,* p. 47.
57. Carter, *Osborne,* pp. 54–55.
58. *Look Back in Anger,* p. 58.
59. Ibid., p. 63.
60. Ibid.
61. Ibid., p. 75.
62. Ibid., p. 77.
63. Worth, "Angry Young Man," p. 155.
64. *Look Back in Anger,* p. 90.
65. Ronald Hayman, *John Osborne* (London, 1968), p. 22.
66. Carter, *Osborne,* p. 61.
67. *Casebook,* pp. 29–30.
68. Ibid., p. 193.
69. Ibid., p. 17. The reviews are collected in the *Casebook*; see also John Elsom's *Post-War British Theatre Criticism* (London: Routledge & Kegan Paul, 1981), pp. 74–80.
70. *Casebook,* p. 173.
71. Ibid., p. 170.
72. Arthur Schlesinger, "Look Back in Amazement," *New Republic* 137 (23 December 1957), pp. 19–21.
73. Leslie Corina, "Still Looking Back," New Republic 138 (10 February 1958), p. 22.
74. Gordon Rogoff, "British Theatre: 1955–66," *Tulane Drama Review* 34 (Winter 1966):31.
75. *Casebook,* pp. 49–51.
76. Ibid., p. 47.
77. See "The Kitchen Sink," *Encounter* 21, no. 6 (December 1963).
78. "A New Word," *Harper's Bazaar,* April 1958, reprinted in *Sights and Spectacles* (London: William Heinemann, 1959), pp. 184–96, and *Casebook,* pp. 150–60.
79. M. C. Bradbrook, *English Dramatic Form* (London: Chatto & Windus, 1965), pp. 186–87.

80. "Osborne's Backward Half-Way Look," *Modern Drama,* no. 6 (1963), pp. 20–25.

81. D. Faber, "The Character of Jimmy Porter: An Approach to *Look Back in Anger,"* Modern Drama 13 (1970–71):67–77.

82. See whole discussion: A. E. Dyson, *"Look Back in Anger," Critical Quarterly* 1, no. 5 (1959):318–26.

83. Elsom, *Post-War British Theatre,* p. 77.

84. *Plays and Players,* January 1969.

85. "They Call It Cricket," pp. 69–70.

86. *Sunday Times,* 24 November 1974.

87. Billington, *Modern Actor,* p. 164.

Chapter Two

1. Walter Kerr, *Tragedy and Comedy* (London: Bodley Head, 1968), p. 326.

2. T. S. Eliot, "The Possibility of a Poetic Drama," in *The Sacred Wood* 1920. Reprint. London: Methuen & Co., 1976), p. 70.

3. Peter Davison, "Contemporary Drama and Popular Dramatic Forms," a lecture delivered 6 November 1963 and published in *Aspects of Drama and the Theatre* (Sydney: Sydney University Press, 1965), pp. 145–97.

4. Editors' introduction, *Encore Reader,* pp. 218–19.

5. *Brecht on Theatre,* ed. and trans. John Willett (London: Eyre Methuen, 1964), p. 227.

6. Quoted in Banham, *Osborne,* p. 30, and *A Better Class of Person,* p. 27.

7. *Anger and After,* pp. 47, 50.

8. *Olivier,* ed. Logan Gourlay (London: Weidenfeld & Nicolson, 1973), p. 145.

9. See Findlater, *Theatrical Censorship in Britain,* pp. 214–15.

10. Richard Findlater, *The Player Kings* (London: Weidenfeld & Nicolson, 1971), pp. 228–29.

11. Banham, *Osborne,* p. 36.

12. Hayman, *British Theatre Since 1955,* pp. 10–11.

13. *Writers' Theatre,* ed. Willis Hall and Keith Waterhouse (London: Heinemann Educational Books, 1967), p. 51.

14. *The Entertainer* (London, 1957), p. 79.

15. Ibid., p. 34.

16. Ibid., p. 51.

17. Ibid., pp. 70–71. Is Osborne recalling Sartre? Nausea disappears when Roquentin hears a negress sing "Some of These Days," *Nausea,* trans. Lloyd Alexander (London: Hamish Hamilton, 1962), p. 34.

18. *The Entertainer,* p. 78.

19. Ibid., p. 83.
20. Ibid., p. 85.
21. *Tynan on Theatre,* p. 49.
22. *New York Times,* 13 and 25 February 1958.
23. *Illustrated London News* 230 (27 April 1957); 231 (28 September 1957); *World Theatre* 6 (Summer 1957).
24. *Sunday Times,* 24 November 1974.
25. *Nation* 186 (1 March 1958).
26. *New York Daily Mirror,* 13 February 1958.
27. *New Statesman,* 11 May 1957.
28. Sheridan Morley, *The Theatre Addict's Archive* (London: Hamish Hamilton, 1977), p. 155.
29. Carter, *John Osborne,* p. 66.
30. Katharine J. Worth, *Revolutions in Modern English Drama* (London, 1973), pp. 75–76.
31. Quoted in Banham, *Osborne,* p. 37.
32. *A Better Class of Person,* p. 257.
33. Nicoll, "Somewhat in a New Dimension," pp. 77–95.
34. *Epitaph for George Dillon* (London, 1958), p. 17.
35. Ibid., p. 29.
36. Ibid., p. 50.
37. Ibid., p. 55.
38. Ibid., pp. 56–57.
39. Ibid., p. 61.
40. Ibid., p. 87.
41. Ibid., p. 41.
42. Ibid., p. 61.
43. Ibid., p. 73.
44. Ibid., p. 75.
45. Trussler, *Plays of Osborne,* p. 38.
46. *New York Daily Mirror,* 2 October 1957.
47. Ibid., 13 February 1958.
48. Ibid., 5 November 1958.
49. Robert Brustein, "Theatre Chronicle," *Hudson Review* 12 (1959–60), pp. 98–101.
50. *Anger and After,* p. 47.
51. Charles Marowitz, *Confessions of a Counterfeit Critic* (London: Eyre Methuen, 1973), pp. 45–47.
52. Worth, "Angry Young Man," p. 156.
53. *Tynan on Theatre,* pp. 65–67.
54. Ferrar, *John Osborne,* p. 15.
55. George E. Wellwarth, *The Theater of Protest and Paradox* (New York, 1964), pp. 226–27.
56. Trussler, *Plays of Osborne,* pp. 27–28.

57. G. K. Hunter, "The World of John Osborne," *Critical Quarterly* 3 (1961):77.

58. Trussler, *John Osborne,* p. 16; and Carter, *John Osborne,* p. 35.

59. *The World of Paul Slickey* (London, 1959), p. 56.

60. The letter is printed in Richard Findlater, *Theatrical Censorship in Britain* (London: Panther, 1968), pp. 216–18.

61. Carter, *John Osborne,* p. 35.

62. "Theatre London," *Theatre Arts* 43 (December 1959), p. 20.

63. *The Encore Reader,* pp. 103–5.

64. *Anger and After,* pp. 50–51.

65. Gabriel Gersh, "The Theater of John Osborne," *Modern Drama* 10 (1967–68):140.

66. George E. Wellwarth, *Theater of Protest,* pp. 228–29.

67. Hunter, "The World of John Osborne," pp. 80–81.

68. Michael Anderson, *Anger and Detachment* (London, 1976), p. 27.

Chapter Three

1. Wardle, *Theatres of Devine,* p. 193.

2. "That Awful Museum," p. 66.

3. In 1977 the editors of *Gay News* were successfully prosecuted for blasphemy but they were fined rather than sent to prison.

4. *A Subject of Scandal and Concern* (London, 1961), p. 24.

5. Ibid., pp. 34–35.

6. *Anger and After,* p. 53.

7. *The World of Paul Slickey,* p. 50.

8. "That Awful Museum," pp. 66–67.

9. *Luther* (London, 1961), p. 24.

10. Ibid., pp. 53–54.

11. Ibid., p. 73.

12. Ibid., p. 74.

13. Ibid., p. 100.

14. Carter, *John Osborne,* p. 39.

15. Tynan, *View of the English Stage,* pp. 314–16.

16. E. G. Rupp, "Luther and Mr. Osborne," *Cambridge Quarterly* 1 (1965–66):28–42.

17. Ferrar, *John Osborne,* p. 28.

18. Trussler, *Plays of Osborne,* p. 105.

19. Carter, *John Osborne,* p. 87.

20. M. C. Bradbrook, *English Dramatic Form* (London: Chatto and Windus, 1965), pp. 187–88.

21. John Simons, "Theatre Chronicle," *Hudson Review* 16 (1963–64): 584–85.

22. Henry Popkin, "Brechtian Europe," *Tulane Drama Review,* no. 37 (Fall 1967), pp. 156–57.

23. Trussler, *Plays of Osborne,* p. 96 ff.
24. *Anger and After,* p. 55.
25. Martin Esslin, "Brecht and the English Theater," in *Brief Chronicles* (London: Maurice Temple Smith, 1970), pp. 84–96.

Chapter Four

1. *The Playwrights Speak,* ed. Walter Wager (London: Longmans Green & Co., 1969), pp. 84–85; both letters are reprinted in the *Casebook.*
2. Ferrar, *John Osborne,* p. 29.
3. Arnold Wesker, *The Friends* (London: Jonathan Cape, 1970), p. 46. Compare also the use of the word in Worth's *Revolutions in Modern English Drama.*
4. Banham, *Osborne,* p. 61.
5. "They Call It Cricket," p. 67.
6. Ibid., p. 76.
7. Ibid.
8. *Plays for England* (London, 1963), p. 33.
9. Ibid., p. 69.
10. See *Directors' Theatre,* ed. Judith Cook (London: George G. Harrap and Co., 1974), p. 99.
11. *Plays for England,* p. 89.
12. Ibid., p. 136.
13. Tynan, *View of the English Stage,* pp. 340–41.
14. Gersh, "Theater of John Osborne," p. 142.
15. Worth, *Revolutions in Modern English Drama,* pp. 77–78.
16. Carter, *John Osborne,* p. 134.
17. Marowitz, *Confessions of a Counterfeit Critic,* p. 60.
18. *The Playwrights Speak,* p. 82, and "They Call It Cricket," p. 77.
19. "They Call It Cricket," p. 65.
20. "That Awful Museum," p. 66.
21. *Sunday Times,* 1 March 1981.
22. *Anger and After* (rev. ed., 1963), p. 55, and *Sunday Times,* 1 March 1981.
23. American readers may have the revised edition published by Grove Press, Inc. This text, with 200 illustrations, was prepared by Robert Hughes to make the script accord with the film, and Osborne was delighted with it.
24. *Tom Jones* (New York and London, 1964), p. 36.
25. Ibid., p. 98.
26. See M. C. Battestin, "Osborne's *Tom Jones*: Adapting a Classic," *Virginia Quarterly* 42 (1966):378–93; reprinted in *Man and the Movies,* ed. W. R. Robinson (Baton Rouge: University of Louisiana Press, 1968), pp. 31–45.

Chapter Five

1. *Anger and After* (rev. ed., 1963), p. 58.
2. *Sunday Times,* 1 March 1981.
3. *The Playwrights Speak,* p. 80.
4. Trussler, *Plays of Osborne,* p. 121.
5. *Inadmissible Evidence* (London, 1965), pp. 9–17.
6. Ibid., p. 20.
7. Kennedy, *Six Dramatists,* p. 199.
8. "They Call It Cricket," p. 81.
9. *Inadmissible Evidence,* p. 55.
10. Robert Brustein, "The English Stage," in *The Third Theatre* (London: Jonathan Cape, 1970), pp. 123–30.
11. Carter, *John Osborne,* p. 90.
12. *Inadmissible Evidence,* p. 59.
13. Ibid., pp. 65–66.
14. Ibid., p. 88.
15. Ibid., p. 106.
16. Trussler, *Plays of Osborne,* p. 137.
17. Ferrar, *John Osborne,* pp. 33–34.
18. Kerr, *Tragedy and Comedy,* pp. 294–95.
19. Laurence Kitchin, "The Wages of Sex," in *Drama in the Sixties* (London, 1966), pp. 189–91.
20. *The Third Theatre,* pp. 146–48.
21. Wardle, *Theatres of Devine,* pp. 272 ff.; Terry Browne, *Playwrights' Theatre,* pp. 59 ff.
22. *A Patriot for Me* (London, 1966), p. 77.
23. Ibid., p. 88.
24. Trussler, *Plays of Osborne,* p. 143.
25. *A Patriot for Me,* p. 118.
26. Ferrar, *John Osborne,* pp. 35–36.
27. Esslin, "Brecht and the English Theatre," pp. 93–94.
28. Worth, *Revolutions in Modern English Drama,* pp. 81–82.
29. Elsom, *Post-War British Theatre,* p. 79.
30. "On Critics and Criticism," *Casebook,* p. 70.
31. *A Bond Honoured* (London, 1966), p. 38.
32. Ibid., p. 43.
33. Ibid., p. 63.
34. Ferrar, *John Osborne,* pp. 37, 38.
35. Trussler, *John Osborne,* p. 25.
36. Anderson, *Anger and Detachment,* p. 31.
37. Trussler, *Plays of Osborne,* p. 151.
38. Reviews by Wardle, Darlington, Hobson, Bryden, and Jones are collected in *Contemporary Theatre,* ed. Geoffrey Morgan (London: London Magazine editions, no. 19, 1968), pp. 21–26.

39. Quoted in Marowitz, *Confessions of a Counterfeit Critic,* p. 111.

40. Daniel Rogers, " 'Not for insolence, but seriously'; John Osborne's adaptation of *La Fianza Satisfecha,*" *Durham University Journal* 60, new series 29 (1967–68):146–70.

Chapter Six

1. Carter, *John Osborne,* p. 45.
2. John Lahr, "Poor Johnny One-Note," reprinted in *Theatre 72,* ed. Sheridan Morley (London, 1972), pp. 185–97.
3. D. L. Hirst, *Comedy of Manners* (London, 1979), p. 86.
4. *Time Present* (London, 1968), p. 16.
5. Ibid., p. 33.
6. Ibid., pp. 46–47.
7. Ibid., p. 41.
8. Worth, *Revolutions in Modern English Drama,* pp. 67–68.
9. Trussler, *Plays of Osborne,* pp. 162–65.
10. Worth, *Revolutions in Modern English Drama,* p. 80.
11. *Time Present,* p. 70.
12. Ferrar, *John Osborne,* p. 39.
13. Lahr, "Poor Johnny One-Note," p. 190.
14. *Anger and After,* pp. 65–66.
15. Kennedy, *Six Dramatists,* pp. 206–7.
16. Carter, *John Osborne,* p. 47.
17. Trussler, *Plays of Osborne,* pp. 222–23.
18. *The Hotel in Amsterdam* (London, 1968), p. 93.
19. Ibid., p. 100.
20. Ibid., p. 99.
21. Ibid., p. 98.
22. Anderson, *Anger and Detachment,* pp. 42–43.
23. *Anger and After,* p. 66.
24. Worth, *Revolutions in Modern English Drama,* pp. 80–81.
25. Lahr, "Poor Johnny One-Note," p. 180.
26. *Sunday Telegraph,* 7 July 1968.
27. Hirst, *Comedy of Manners,* pp. 79–81.
28. Interview with Keith Dewhurst, *Evening Standard,* 6 December 1971.
29. Ibid.
30. *West of Suez* (London, 1971), p. 54.
31. Ibid., p. 22.
32. *New Standard,* 6 March 1981.
33. *West of Suez,* pp. 74, 77.
34. Ibid., p. 84.
35. *Sunday Times,* 1 March 1981.
36. Anderson, *Anger and Detachment,* p. 46.

37. Lahr, "Poor Johnny One-Note," p. 196.
38. Hirst, *Comedy of Manners,* p. 93.
39. Worth, *Revolutions in Modern English Drama,* p. 75.
40. Sheridan Morley, *Review Copies* (London: Robson Books, 1947), pp. 87–88.
41. John Edmunds, *New Theatre Magazine* 12, no. 2 (n.d.):36.

Chapter Seven

1. Billington, *Modern Actor,* p. 171.
2. Browne, *Playwrights' Theatre,* p. 99.
3. Anderson, *Anger and Detachment,* p. 48.
4. "That Awful Museum," p. 65.
5. *A Better Class of Person,* p. 276.
6. *A Sense of Detachment* (London, 1973), pp. 14–15.
7. Ibid., p. 58.
8. Morley, *Review Copies,* pp. 157–69.
9. *New Standard,* 7 April 1981.
10. *Sunday Times,* 24 November 1974.
11. *The Entertainer,* p. 61.
12. *The End of Me Old Cigar* (London, 1975), p. 41.
13. *Sunday Times,* 19 January 1975.
14. Quoted in John Lahr, "Poor Johnny One-Note," p. 188.
15. *Watch It All Come Down* (London, 1975), p. 12.
16. Ibid., pp. 16–17.
17. Ibid., p. 51.
18. Hunter, "The World of John Osborne," p. 81.

Chapter Eight

1. *Hedda Gabler* (London, 1972), p. 8.
2. *Observer,* 2 July 1972.
3. Morley, *Review Copies,* pp. 131–32.
4. *A Place Calling Itself Rome* (London, 1973), p. 20.
5. Ibid., p. 50.
6. Ibid., p. 63.
7. Ibid., p. 77.
8. *The Picture of Dorian Gray* (London, 1973), p. 11.
9. Ibid., p. 12.
10. Anderson, *Anger and Detachment,* p. 31.
11. J. R. Taylor in *The Revels History of Drama in English* (London: Methuen & Co., 1978), 7:239.
12. *New Standard,* 6 March 1981.
13. *Sunday Times,* 1 March 1981.
14. *The Right Prospectus* (London, 1970), p. 16.

15. Ibid., p. 19.
16. Ibid., pp. 24–25.
17. Ibid., p. 45.
18. *The Times,* 23 October 1970.
19. Ferrar, *John Osborne,* pp. 43–44.
20. Worth, *Revolutions in Modern English Drama,* p. 69.
21. *The End of Me Old Cigar,* pp. 64–65.
22. *Observer,* 7 July 1968.
23. Anderson, *Anger and Detachment,* p. 29.
24. Ibid., p. 32.
25. *The Gift of Friendship* (London, 1972), p. 28. Or the Gospel according to Webber and Rice. *Jesus Christ—Superstar* appeared in 1970.
26. *The Gift of Friendship,* p. 33.
27. Ibid., p. 35.
28. *Sunday Times,* 27 January 1980.
29. *Try a Little Tenderness* (London, 1978), p. 55.

Chapter Nine

1. *Observer,* 4 July 1965; 30 June and 7 July 1968.
2. *The Times,* 14 October 1967.
3. John Whiting, "At Ease in a Bright Red Tie," in *Encore Reader,* p. 107.
4. Gersh, "Theater of John Osborne."
5. *New Standard,* 27 and 6 March 1981.
6. *Sunday Times,* 1 March 1981.

Selected Bibliography

PRIMARY SOURCES

1. Books

Look Back in Anger. London: Faber & Faber, 1957.

The Entertainer. London: Faber & Faber, 1957.

Epitaph for George Dillon (in collaboration with Anthony Creighton). London: Faber & Faber, 1958.

The World of Paul Slickey. London: Faber & Faber, 1959.

A Subject of Scandal and Concern. London: Faber & Faber, 1961.

Luther. London: Faber & Faber, 1961.

Plays for England (The Blood of the Bambergs and *Under Plain Cover)*. London: Faber & Faber, 1963.

Tom Jones: A Screenplay. London: Faber & Faber, 1964; revised edition, New York: Grove Press, 1964.

Inadmissible Evidence. London: Faber & Faber, 1965.

A Patriot for Me. London: Faber & Faber, 1966.

A Bond Honoured. London: Faber & Faber, 1966.

Time Present and *The Hotel in Amsterdam*. London: Faber & Faber, 1968.

The Right Prospectus: A Play for Television. London: Faber & Faber, 1970.

West of Suez. London: Faber & Faber, 1971.

Very Like A Whale. London: Faber & Faber, 1971.

Hedda Gabler (adapted by John Osborne). London: Faber & Faber, 1972.

The Gift of Friendship: A Play for Television. London: Faber & Faber, 1972.

A Sense of Detachment. London: Faber & Faber, 1973.

A Place Calling Itself Rome. London: Faber & Faber, 1973.

The Picture of Dorian Gray (adapted from the novel by Oscar Wilde). London: Faber & Faber, 1973.

The End of Me Old Cigar (and *Jill and Jack*). London: Faber & Faber, 1975.

Watch It Come Down. London: Faber & Faber, 1975.

You're Not Watching Me, Mummy and Try A Little Tenderness: Two Plays for Television. London: Faber & Faber, 1978.

A Better Class of Person: An Autobiography: 1929–1956. London and Boston: Faber & Faber, 1981.

2. Articles

"Sex and Failure." *Observer*, 20 January 1957. Reprinted in *Protest*. Edited by Gene Feldman and Max Gartenberg, 1960, 269–71.

"The Writer in His Age." *London Magazine* 4 (May 1957):47–49. Reprinted in *Casebook* 59–62.

"They Call It Cricket." In: *Declaration.* Edited by Tom Maschler, 1957, 63–84. Extracts reprinted in *Playwrights on Playwriting.* Edited by Toby Cole, 1960.

"Introduction" to *International Theatre Annual,* II. Edited by Harold Hobson, 1957, 9–10.

"Come On In: The Revolution is Only Just Beginning." *Tribune,* 27 March 1959.

"The Epistle to the Philistines." *Tribune,* 13 May 1960. Reprinted in *Casebook,* 62–63.

"That Awful Museum." *Twentieth Century Literature* 169 (February 1961):212–16. Reprinted in *Casebook,* 63–67.

"A Letter to My Fellow Countrymen." *Tribune,* 18 August 1961. Reprinted in *Casebook,* 67–69.

"The Pioneer at the Royal Court: George Devine." *Observer,* 23 January 1966.

"On Critics and Criticism." *Sunday Telegraph,* 28 August 1966. Reprinted in *Casebook,* 69–71.

"On the thesis business and the seekers after the Bare Approximate; on the rights of the audience and the wink and the promise of the well-made play." *The Times,* 14 October 1967.

3. Interviews

In *The Playwrights Speak.* Edited by Walter Wager, 1967, 90–109. An edited version of an interview given to John Freeman in "Face to Face," broadcast on BBC Television, 21 January 1962.

In the *Observer,* 30 June and 7 July 1968. Interview, in two parts, with Kenneth Tynan.

In *Evening Standard,* 6 December 1971. "What Osborne Saw West of Suez." Interview with Keith Dewhurst.

In *Sunday Times,* 24 November 1974. "Jester Flees the Court." Interview with Mark Amory.

In the *Observer,* 18 November 1979. "Fifty is a young age for an Angry Man." Interview with Robert Chesshyre.

In *Sunday Times,* 1 March 1981. "Middle Age of the Angry Young Men." Interview with W. J. Weatherby.

In the *New Standard,* 6 March 1981. "A Better Class of Osborne." Interview with Valerie Grove.

In: *At the Royal Court: 25 Years of the English Stage Company.* Edited by Richard Findlater (Derbyshire: Ambergate, 1981): "On the Writer's Side," in conversation with Richard Findlater, Derbyshire: Ambergate, pp. 19–26.

SECONDARY SOURCES

1. Bibliographies

Bailey, Shirley J. "John Osborne: A Bibliography." *Twentieth Century Literature* 7 (1961):118–20.

Palmer, Helen H., and Dyson, Anne J. "John James Osborne." *European Drama Criticism,* 1968, pp. 305–10.

These are useful for finding out where reviews of original London and New York productions appeared in periodical publications and newspapers. They have been largely superseded by:

Northouse, Cameron, and Walsh, Thomas P. *John Osborne: A Reference Guide.* Boston: G. K. Hall & Co., 1974. This aims to cover the career of John Osborne from 1956–1972 by listing his work and the response to that work. It is by no means complete but it offers, through its annotated entries, a fair guide to Osborne criticism.

2. Symposium

Taylor, John Russell, ed. *John Osborne: Look Back in Anger: A Casebook.* London: Macmillan & Co., 1968. Provides reviews of the first performance, five prose works by Osborne, critical studies, and some foreign reviews. Taylor gives an overall picture of the context in his introduction and A. E. Dyson presents his response to the play in the "General Editor's Comments."

3. Books on Osborne

Banham, Martin. *Osborne.* Edinburgh: Oliver & Boyd, 1969. Comment on individual plays up to *The Hotel in Amsterdam.* Banham argues that Osborne's importance is greater than the success of any play. It was he who "overnight brought the English theatre up-to-date" and restored it once more to "the arena of controversy."

Carter, Alan. *John Osborne.* Edinburgh: Oliver & Boyd, 1969. A biographical chapter is followed by a chapter on the response to the plays. Carter divides the plays (to *The Hotel in Amsterdam*) into "Public" and "Private" Voice and argues that Osborne is working on the formula: Anger = Care = Love. Thus Carter sees Osborne as a very positive idealist who cares for humanity and the conditions in which it lives.

Ferrar, Harold. *John Osborne.* New York & London: Columbia University Press, 1973. An essay briefly covering Osborne's work up to *West of Suez.* Ferrar concludes that it is difficult to write about a playwright whose demands are "almost solely on the store of our human sympathy" and who is, essentially, a man of the theater, and particularly of an actor's theater.

Hayman, Ronald. *John Osborne.* London: Heinemann, 1968. Each chapter examines an individual play to *A Bond Honoured* and Hayman concludes that there is an incomplete fusion of the personal and public elements. His influence on the English theater is undeniable but as a dramatist he has not yet written a play that can be praised except in terms of particular moments or scenes. Revised in 1972, the book now covers the plays to *West of Suez*.

Trussler, Simon. *John Osborne*. Writers and Their Work: No. 213. London: Longmans, Green & Co., 1969.

———. *The Plays of John Osborne*. London: Gollancz, 1969. Analyses of all Osborne's plays to *The Hotel in Amsterdam* with little attempt to trace recurring themes or stylistic development. Trussler hoped that the book would stimulate serious debate about Osborne and looks at the texts as the "raw material of productions." A chronology, cast lists, and bibliography are provided.

4. General Works

Anderson, Michael. *Anger and Detachment*. London: Pitman Publishing, 1976. Looks briefly at the later development of Osborne, Pinter, and John Arden asking whether they have maintained the impetus of their early work. Anderson suggests that Osborne has achieved an easier conversational style and more accurate pictures of England, one of his major themes. See chapters 1 and 2.

Billington, Michael. *The Modern Actor*. London: Hamish Hamilton, 1973. See pp. 162–71.

Brown, J. R. *Theatre Language*. London: Penguin Press, 1972. A study of Arden, Osborne, Pinter, and Wesker. Theater language means any kind of expression that theater can use and control. See chapter 4.

Elsom, John. *Post-War British Theatre*. London: Routledge & Kegan Paul, 1976. See Chapter 5, pp. 72–81, where Elsom looks at Osborne's work to *The End of Me Old Cigar*.

Evans, Gareth Lloyd. *The Language of Modern Drama*. London: J. M. Dent & Sons, 1977. Discusses the way a playwright uses words in a theatrical context. Covers a wide range of dramatists starting with Shaw. See pp. 102–13.

Hayman, Ronald. *British Theatre Since 1955: A Reassessment*. Oxford: Oxford University Press, 1979. Looks at what has been achieved in British theater since 1955, the date of *Waiting for Godot*. The brief discussion of Osborne concentrates on his problem in writing for the physical shape of the Royal Court. See pp. 34–38.

Hewison, Robert. *In Anger*. London: Weidenfeld & Nicolson, 1981. As its subtitle—Culture in the Cold War 1945–60—implies, Hewison looks at the way in which the ground was prepared for Osborne and the context, political and cultural, in which he wrote.

Hirst, D. L. *Comedy of Manners*. London: Methuen & Co., 1979. A short and possibly idiosyncratic survey of the genre from Ben Jonson to the present day. The section on Osborne concentrates on plays since *Time Present* as examples of comedies of manners. See pp. 81–96.

Kennedy, Andrew. *Six Dramatists in Search of a Language.* Cambridge: Cambridge University Press, 1975. Chapter 5 looks at Osborne.

Kitchin, Laurence. *Drama in the Sixties.* London: Faber & Faber, 1966. See the essays "Redbrick Luther" and "The Wages of Sex," pp. 185–91.

Mander, John. *The Writer and Commitment.* London: Secker & Warburg, 1961. If not entirely satisfactory it tackles a crucial topic; the introduction and pp. 181–88 are useful discussions of commitment, art, and anger.

Marowitz, Charles, with Milne, Tom, and Hale, Owen. *The Encore Reader.* London: Methuen & Co., 1965. An anthology from the theater magazine *Encore* covering the period 1956–63. Invaluable.

Taylor, J. R. *Anger and After.* London: Methuen & Co., 1969. This guide to the new British drama starts, as its title implies, in 1956 with *Look Back in Anger.* Osborne's work is described, to *The Hotel in Amsterdam,* on pp. 39–66. See also revised version in *Casebook,* pp. 75–96.

Tynan, Kenneth. *Curtains.* London: Longmans, Green & Co., 1961. Revised edition: *Tynan on Theatre.* Harmondsworth: Penguin Books, Ltd., 1964.

———. *A View of the English Stage.* Frogmore: Granada Publishing, 1976. Both these volumes are collections of reviews by possibly the liveliest dramatic critic of the period. Apart from reviews of Osborne's plays they give some idea of the plays against which Osborne was measured.

Wardle, Irving. *The Theatres of George Devine.* London: Jonathan Cape, 1978. Osborne insisted that his relationship with Devine was a private one and refused to provide copy for this study. Devine was a founder member of the English Stage Company and the book remains invaluable. Chapters 11 on are relevant to any study of Osborne.

Wellwarth, George E. *The Theater of Protest and Paradox.* New York: New York University, 1964. Although revised this first edition remains valuable as an immediate response to Osborne by an American, covering the plays to *Plays for England.* See pp. 222–34.

Williams, Raymond. *Drama from Ibsen to Brecht.* London: Chatto & Windus, 1968. See *"Look Back in Anger:* John Osborne," pp. 318–22.

Worth, Katharine J. *Revolutions in Modern English Drama.* London: G. Bell & Sons, 1973. "Revolutions" here mean the turning of the wheel that brings up the past in new forms. Osborne is seen as inheriting the comic patterns of Shaw and Coward. See Chapter 5.

5. Articles

Bode, Carl. *"The Redbrick Cinderellas." College English* 20, no. 7 (April 1959): 331–37. A stimulating essay by an American in England on the angry young men—Osborne, Amis, and Wain.

Deming, Barbara. "John Osborne's War Against the Philistines." *Hudson Review* 11 (1958–59): 411–19. Criticism on both *Look Back in Anger* and *The Entertainer* largely prompted by Mary McCarthy's claims for Osborne in "A New Word." Deming disagrees with McCarthy's praise of Osborne as a reformer whose anger is intended to waken up the complacent. She finds Osborne's anger itself a form of complacent snobbery and an intrusion in the drama.

Dyson, A. E. "Look Back in Anger." *Critical Quarterly* 1 (1959): 318–26. Examines the mixed nature of Jimmy Porter and his relationship with Osborne.

Faber, M. D. "The Character of Jimmy Porter: An Approach to *Look Back in Anger*." *Modern Drama* 13 (1970–71): 67–77. A psychoanalytical approach to *Look Back in Anger* showing that it is only an antiestablishment play in part. What it really presents us with "is an orally fixated neurotic who projects his own psychological shortcomings onto the external environment."

Gersh, Gabriel. "The Theater of John Osborne." *Modern Drama* 10 (September 1967): 137–43. Excellent review of Osborne's plays to 1968 looking at his search for style and the quality of his social concern.

Huss, Roy. "John Osborne's Backward Half-Way Look." *Modern Drama* 6 (1963): 20–25. Looks at the "unresolved Oedipal situation" in which Jimmy Porter is enmeshed.

Lahr, John. "Poor Johnny One-Note." *Evergreen Review* 12 (December 1968): 61–63, 93–95. Reprinted in *Up Against the Fourth Wall.* New York: Grove Press, 1970, and *Theatre 72.* Edited by Sheridan Morley. London: Hutchinson & Co., Ltd., 1972, pp. 185–97. A lively essay which argues that as Osborne has grown successful he has grown less angry and dramatically flabby. As my text shows, I hope, I think Lahr is deaf to the tones of English conversation.

Marowitz, Charles. "The Ascension of John Osborne." *Tulane Drama Review* 6 (Winter 1962): 55–68. Reprinted in *Casebook,* pp. 161–65. Looks at religious skepticism in Osborne's plays and suggests Brechtian influence in *Luther.*

McCarthy, Mary. "A New Word." *Harper's Bazaar,* April 1958. Reprinted in *Sights and Spectacles,* 1959, 184–96, and *Casebook,* 150–60. Sees Osborne as primarily a social critic who gives modern society with its evils and repression of the individual a new word: hell.

Nicoll, Allardyce. "Somewhat in a New Dimension." *Contemporary Theatre.* Edited by J. R. Brown and B. Harris. London: Stratford-upon-Avon Studies, No. 4, 1962, pp. 77–95. Looks at Osborne in relation to earlier dramatists.

Rogers, Daniel. " 'Not for Insolence, but Seriously': John Osborne's adaptation of *La fianza satisfecha.*" *Durham University Journal* 60, n.s. 29 (1967–68): 146–70. Detailed look at Osborne's adaptation and the original by an Hispanist who is more enthusiastic about the result than most critics.

Rogoff, Gordon. "Richard's Himself Again: Journey to an Actors' Theatre." *Tulane Drama Review* 11 (1966): 29–40. Osborne is more a figure from the past than the present who only seemed to be a revolutionary dramatist and who only seemed to start a movement.

Rupp, E. G. "John Osborne and the Historical Luther." *Expository Times* 73 (February 1962): 147–51. Comments on historical chronology of play and shows Osborne's dependence on Erik Erikson.

Rupp, E. G. "Luther and Mr. Osborne." *Cambridge Quarterly* 1 (1965): 28–42. Article stimulated by Manchester production of *Luther.* Looks at historical Luther, the use of Erik Erikson, and comments on success of Osborne's treatment.

Taylor, J. R. "Ten Years of the English Stage Company." *Tulane Drama Review* 11 (1966):120–31. The ten years start, more or less, with *Look Back in Anger.*

Wardle, Irving. "Osborne and the Critics." *New Society,* 16 June 1966, pp. 22–23. Discusses Osborne's response to criticism of *A Bond Honoured.* Wardle feels Osborne should discuss his differences with critics but praises him as the best dramatist of the day.

Worth, Katharine J. "The Angry Young Man: John Osborne." *Experimental Drama.* Edited by William A. Armstrong. London: Hutchinson, 1963. Reprinted in *Casebook,* 101–16. Looks at Osborne's career and traces themes in plays to *Luther* showing an affinity in the early plays with the theater of Shaw and Galsworthy. Osborne begins to be more innovative and develops into a more competent dramatist.

Index

Amis, Kingsley, *Lucky Jim*, 9
Artaud, Antonin, 5

Bagnold, Enid, *The Chalk Garden,* 6
Beckett, Samuel, 5, 18, 48, 59–60; *Waiting for Godot,* 94
Brecht, Bertolt, 5, 28–29, 49, 51, 120; *Galileo,* 57, 58–59

Chekhov, Anton, 38, 106
Coward, Noël, 8, 56, 62, 99, 106; *The Vortex,* 5; *Fumed Oak,* 42

Dean, James, *Rebel Without A Cause,* 8
Dennis, Nigel, *Cards of Identity,* 6
Devine, George, 4, 5, 65, 77, 83
Duncan, Ronald, *Don Juan,* 6

Eliot, T.S., 6, 27
Erikson, Erik H., *Young Man Luther,* 57

Fielding, Henry, 105; *Tom Jones,* 68–70
Finney, Albert, 52, 68

Gay, John, 48

Handke, Peter, *Publikumsbeschimpfung,* 107
Hawkins, Anthony Hope, *The Prisoner of Zenda,* 62

Ibsen, Henrik, *Hedda Gabler,* 116–17, 123
Irving, Henry, *The Bells,* 73

Kipling, Rudyard, 31, 100, 112

Miller, Arthur, 20, 30
Miller, Jonathan, 65

Olivier, Laurence, 20, 29–31, 35, 36, 37
Orton, Joe, 46
Osborne, John, and Brecht, 28–29, 51, 58–60; and the critics, 45, 86–87, 132; early life, 1–2; early plays, 2–3; and films, 67–68; and homosexuality, 15, 76–86, 122; and the music hall, 26–28; and politics, 8–13, 131; and the Press, 50, 51, 67; and television, 49, 116

ADAPTATIONS:
Bond Honoured, A, 83–88, 132
Hedda Gabler, 116–17
Picture of Dorian Gray, The, 116, 120–23
Place Calling Itself Rome, A, 116, 117–20

FILMS:
Luther, 60
Tom Jones, 61, 67–70

PLAYS:
Blood of the Bambergs, The, 62–64
End of Me Old Cigar, The, 109–12
Entertainer, The, 4, 26–38, 42, 44, 46, 62, 68, 71, 100, 110

Epitaph for George Dillon, 3, 38–44, 56, 84, 89, 99
Hotel in Amsterdam, The, 37, 72, 89, 95–100, 104, 132
Inadmissible Evidence, 42, 43, 68, 71–76, 89, 95, 118, 132
Look Back in Anger, 3, 4, 5, 6, 7, 8, 9, 10, 11, 12, 13–25, 26, 27, 28, 29, 30, 38, 39, 42, 44, 56, 68, 71, 89, 92, 109, 110, 131, 132
Luther, 4, 49, 51–60, 61, 71, 84, 95
Patriot for Me, A, 4, 49, 60, 76–83, 118
Sense of Detachment, A, 107–109, 110
Time Present, 24, 38, 89, 90–95, 98, 106
Under Plain Cover, 65–67, 124
Watch It Come Down, 112–15, 129
West of Suez, 100–106, 109, 113, 126
World of Paul Slickey, The, 44–48, 51, 61, 63, 109, 115

PLAYS FOR TELEVISION:
Gift of Friendship, The, 127–28
Jill and Jack, 124–25
Right Prospectus, The, 123–24
Subject of Scandal and Concern, A, 48–51, 67, 72
Try a Little Tenderness, 129–30
Very Like A Whale, 126–27
You're Not Watching Me, Mummy, 128–29

PROSE:
Better Class of Person, A, 1, 132
"Epistle to the Philistines, The," 61
"Letter to My Fellow Countrymen, A," 61
"Sex and Failure," 13, 116
"The Writer in His Age," 11–12
"They Call It Cricket," 11, 24, 62, 63

Pinter, Harold, 7, 68; *The Lover,* 66

Richardson, Tony, 5, 19, 30, 49, 51, 68
Royal Court Theater, The, 3–5, 77, 109–10, 114, 132

Shakespeare, William, *Coriolanus,* 117–20
Shaw, G. Bernard, 14, 42, 62, 66, 106, 118, 132; *Heartbreak House,* 28, 103, 105; *Mrs. Warren's Profession,* 67
Stevenson, R.L., *Dr. Jekyll and Mr. Hyde,* 120

Wall, Max, 36
Wesker, Arnold, *The Friends,* 62
Wilde, Oscar, 46, 62, 112, 123; *The Picture of Dorian Gray,* 120–23
Williams, Tennessee, 13
Williamson, Nicol, 71

Vega, Lope de, 83; *La Fianza Satisfecha,* 84, 86–88

DATE DUE
